Taxcafe.co.uk Tax Guides

Keeping it Simple

*Small Business Bookkeeping,
Cash Flow, Tax & VAT*

By James Smith BSc FCA

Important Legal Notices:

Taxcafe®
TAX GUIDE – 'Keeping it Simple - Small Business Bookkeeping, Cash Flow, Tax & VAT'

Published by:
Taxcafe UK Limited
67 Milton Road
Kirkcaldy KY1 1TL
United Kingdom
Tel: (01592) 560081

15th Edition June 2018

ISBN   978-1-911020-31-8

Disclaimer
Before reading or relying on the content of this tax guide, please read the disclaimer carefully.

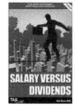

Disclaimer

About the Author

I am a chartered accountant and have been working in general practice for over ten years. Based in Oxfordshire but with clients located across the country, I deal predominantly with small businesses and individuals. I originally trained with KPMG, one of the largest accounting firms in the country, before moving into the 'real world' of industry, taking on a number of roles in both a large manufacturing company and smaller scale service businesses until setting up my own practice in 2002.

If you have any suggestions to make things easier for readers of future editions of this book, I would be very pleased to hear from you.

For more details about my practice, please see my website. Unlike traditional High Street accountants, I can usually deal with most UK tax and business issues wherever you are located.

Contact details

Website   http://www.jamesesmith.co.uk
Email: contact@jamesesmith.co.uk

Dedication

To my grandparents, for your guidance and encouragement.

Contents

Contents (cont...)

Introduction

The purpose of this guide is to help owners of small businesses keep basic accounting records, improve their cash flow, complete a self-assessment tax return and understand VAT.

The bookkeeping and accounting chapters start by going over the basics of record keeping for sole traders and gradually build to take account of your legal responsibilities and information needs.

The self-assessment section takes a guinea pig taxpayer and shows how the 'self-employment' tax return pages can be completed with minimum fuss.

The cash flow section contains numerous tips I have picked up over the years and will help your business get paid on time and make sure the money keeps rolling in.

The VAT section starts at ground level, showing you how VAT operates and helping you decide whether to register voluntarily or wait until you are forced to do so. The book gives practical pointers on how to register for VAT and what VAT scheme options exist to help you. The book ends with some suggested strategies you can use to get the most out of the VAT system.

The earlier sections of the book are useful when you are just starting up. Some of the themes covered later on will probably only become relevant after your first year or two of trading so you should find this book a useful resource for several years to come.

Section 1

Basic Bookkeeping

Chapter 1

How to Keep Basic Records

Although each business must assess its own record needs, there are certain things that apply to all businesses and the following section sets out the fundamentals.

Separation of Business & Personal Accounts

If you have recently started a business the first thing you should do is open a business bank account. This may sound obvious if you have already done so but many people start off using their personal bank accounts. This makes your record keeping that much harder as you will later have to determine whether each transaction was for personal or business reasons and you are unable to control your accounts with good bank reconciliation.

Most banks offer free banking for start-ups (typically for 18 months) and many throw in free advice and other perks. Do pay close attention to the fees once the free period ends, which may either be per transaction or a fixed monthly amount. At the time of writing the only major bank offering longer term free banking was the Co-operative Bank, but this is for Federation of Small Business members only. Generally speaking, 'direct banking' accounts which are run via the internet/post/phone are available at a lower cost than traditional branch-based accounts. If however you like or need to bank over the counter due to handling cash, these accounts will not generally be suitable.

Records of Your Income

Different businesses receive income from different sources. However, the basic principle does not change: you should keep good records that summarise your sources of income.

For a service company that sends out invoices, this record would simply be a list of invoices issued, as depicted in Figure 1.1.

Figure 1.1 Income Spreadsheet

Ref	Description	Date	Amount
INV001	Mr A	05/01/2018	1,000.00
INV002	Mr C	06/01/2018	250.00
Total			**1,250.00**

- 'Ref' is the sequential and unique invoice number.
- 'Description' gives the client name and possibly the work completed.
- 'Date' is the invoice date.
- 'Amount' is the total invoice value.

A good idea is to keep a copy of all the invoices in a ring binder, in sequential order, detailing the work completed. The above spreadsheet would be your summary accounting record.

For a retail business, totals of the daily or weekly till receipts may be appropriate. The following sections discuss in more detail how to amend the basic record above for your own specific business needs, so don't worry too much if the above layout is inappropriate.

Retaining Your Receipts

A receipt is proof that you bought something. HM Revenue & Customs may require this proof to be produced if you are ever investigated. You can submit secondary evidence, such as proof the payment went through your bank account or credit card statement, but you should not rely too heavily on this method of record keeping.

Keeping Your Receipts in Order

If you just throw your receipts in a carrier bag and hope for the best you will always struggle to keep good accounting records. The first step towards improving your records is to convert your carrier bag into some sense of order.

For example:

- Sort out your receipts into rough date order or by month.
- Number them with a thick marker pen starting with '1' for your earliest receipt. Keep this numbering system running forward so every receipt has a unique number on (say) the top right corner.
- Clip together a bundle of receipts (in numerical order) for every week or month.
- Put each bundle in a separate clear plastic wallet to stop them getting lost. It is helpful to indicate on the outside of the wallet the range of receipt numbers.
- Place in a box file or binder.

Processing Your Receipts

Now that you've got your receipts in order it's time to process them using a basic computer spreadsheet or manual accounts book. You may choose to use some accounting software but this will probably be overdoing it if you are just starting out. Figure 1.2 shows the layout for two example purchases: stationery for keeping your records and this book.

Figure 1.2 Expenses Spreadsheet

No.	Date	Payee	Description	Amount	Stationery	Books	Other
1	05/01/2018	Staples	Office Supplies	59.50	59.50		
2	06/01/2018	Taxcafe	Books	24.95		24.95	
				-			
				-			
				-			
				84.45	59.50	24.95	-

- In the first column 'No.' is the receipt number you have written in the top right corner when putting your receipts in order.
- 'Date' is the date of the invoice.
- 'Payee' is the person you bought the item from.
- 'Description' is the type of item you purchased.
- 'Amount' is the amount of the invoice you paid out (VAT is covered in later sections).
- There are now three further columns 'Stationery', 'Books' and 'Other'. These columns are there to describe the *type* of expenditure you incur and are very powerful and one of the keys to keeping good records.

Over time you will end up with a long list of expenses. Using this spreadsheet you will be able to:

- Easily see your total expenditure.

- See the total spend in a period for any type of item, such as stationery, by looking at the total at the bottom of the relevant column. You can insert subtotals to monitor the weekly or monthly performance.

- Find information. If you know you spent money on stationery, for example, but can't recall who the supplier was, you can quickly review the relevant analysis column and find the supplier and price.

- Find a given invoice. All you need do is find the relevant invoice number in the first column. Assuming you have marked up your invoices in numerical sequence and placed them in a box file they should be easy to retrieve without hours of searching.

- Save money. If instead of typing up your expenses yourself you give them to an accountant, they will charge you for this service. Rates vary widely depending on what firm you use and where you live. However, it is not unusual to pay between £15 and £30 an hour to have an accountancy firm type up your expenses.

Important: This section is fundamental to keeping good records. If you aren't happy with the basic principles listed above I strongly recommend you stop and go back over this section again, perhaps completing some worked examples using your own records. The following sections build on a basic working understanding of the above.

Chapter 2

Basic Accounting Controls

This chapter outlines the basic controls or 'checks and balances' that you can use to make sure your accounts are accurate.

Without controls it is very easy for your accounts to become inaccurate and unreliable. Good controls provide 'control loops' that ensure all entries are complete and accurate.

This might sound complex but it is actually straightforward if you take time and are patient about entering your data.

The only real difference between good and bad bookkeeping is the check procedures to ensure mistakes in data entry are quickly spotted and resolved.

Batch Totals

A batch total can be used to check that a group of figures (for example, your monthly expenses) is entered correctly into your accounting records.

In Chapter 1 I outlined a way to keep your receipts bundled – one bundle for every month. By adding up all the invoices in any particular month with a calculator, you can check if this figure matches the total amount appearing in your spreadsheet.

This is your batch total.

I always keep a printed copy of the spreadsheet, listing all the expenses, on the front of my invoice batches. This serves as a useful quick reference.

The more invoices you have the more important this type of procedure is to ensure you don't miss something or make a typing error.

A batch procedure may go something like this:

- Gather up the purchase invoices for the month as described in Chapter 1.
- Enter the invoices into your accounting records, for example using a spreadsheet.
- Add up all the invoices you've typed up (programs like Microsoft Excel let you do this automatically).
- Using a calculator add up all the paper invoices manually to check if the totals are the same.
- If there are any differences between the spreadsheet and the calculator:
  - Print out your spreadsheet for the period showing all the expenses.
  - Tick off line by line the invoices appearing in the spreadsheet against the paper invoices in your batch. As they are (hopefully!) in the same order this should be pretty painless and you will quickly see where the errors are.

Bank Reconciliations

Bank reconciliations are the fundamental control within any accounts system. They ensure that everything that has gone through the bank account is reflected somewhere in the accounts, even if it is in the wrong place. It is, therefore, helpful to get into the habit of doing regular bank reconciliations.

To complete accurate bank reconciliations you need two basic things:

- A separate business bank account so that only business transactions go through the account.
- Good accounting records showing the income and expenditure in the period.

The best time to complete a bank reconciliation is once a month when your bank statement arrives in the post. The worst time to do one is at the end of the financial year, having not completed one all year.

'Little and often' is the golden rule of good business bookkeeping.

Figure 2.1 shows how a simple bank reconciliation would look.

Figure 2.1 Bank Reconciliation

Opening bank balance as at 1st January 2018		500.00
Less purchases in the period		(84.45)
Add sales Income in the period		1,250.00
Closing balance expected 31st January 2018		1,665.55
Actual balance on the bank statement		1,660.55
Difference		(5.00)

We take the opening balance from the last time a reconciliation was completed (in this case the 1st of January), deduct the known purchases listed in the expenses spreadsheet, add the sales income from the sales spreadsheet and calculate an expected closing balance.

Looking at the actual balance on the bank statement you can see that the totals don't quite match up. Now £5 might not sound like much but there could be several things going wrong both ways – in other words, missed income AND missed expenditure.

First, take a good look at your bank statement. Figure 2.2 is a sample bank statement which contains the following transactions:

Figure 2.2 Bank Statement

Any Bank Account			Payments	Receipts	Balance
1 Jan 2018	Brought Forward				500.00
7 Jan 2018	Switch		59.50		440.50
9 Jan 2018	Switch		24.95		415.55
15 Jan 2018	Cheque			1,000.00	1,415.55
17 Jan 2018	Cheque			250.00	1,665.55
19 Jan 2018	Cheque			100.00	1,765.55
22 Jan 2018	Transfer		105.00		1,660.55
	Closing Balance				1,660.55

At this point a lot of people give up, especially in a real-life scenario where the bank statement contains dozens of items and the apparent difference is very small. However, if your records have been prepared as described above, you should be able to quickly find the problem.

First, compare the payments in your bank statement with the list of expenses on your spreadsheet.

You can quickly tick off the £59.50 and the £24.95 but there is also a mystery payment of £105 on 22 January. You quickly realise that this amount was money taken out as a 'drawing'.

Drawings are amounts taken personally by the owner of a sole trader business. Strictly speaking they are not a business expense, but recording them on your expenses sheet makes sense for bookkeeping purposes.

You therefore go back and amend the 'expenses' spreadsheet adding a descriptive column for 'drawings' (Figure 2.3)

Figure 2.3 Expenses Spreadsheet

No.	Date	Payee	Description	Amount	Stationery	Books	Drawings
1	05/01/2018	Staples	Office Supplies	59.50	59.50		
2	06/01/2018	Taxcafe	Books	24.95		24.95	
3	22/01/2018	Self	Drawings	105.00			105.00
				-			
				-			
				189.45	59.50	24.95	105.00

A similar review of the sales income shows a mystery cheque for £100 deposited in the bank. Then you recall that you had completed three items of work in January and had forgotten to list the third invoice and update the sales list accordingly.

The revised reconciliation is as follows (Figure 2.4):

Figure 2.4 Bank Reconciliation

Opening bank balance as at 1st January 2018		500.00
Less purchases in the period		(189.45)
Add sales income in the period		1,350.00
Closing balance expected 31st January 2018		1,660.55
Actual balance on the bank statement		1,660.55
Difference		0.00

There is now no difference showing between the bank statement and the spreadsheet and the accounts are therefore fully reconciled.

Sometimes there are genuine differences between your cash position and what is shown in your accounts.

Typical reasons for this would be:

- Sales invoices that haven't been paid yet.
- Things you have bought but not paid for yet.
- Cheques you have paid into the bank account but haven't cleared.
- Personal items purchased from the business account.
- Business items purchased from private funds.

In these circumstances you may have some 'reconciling items'.

Some of these, such as invoices not yet paid and uncleared cheques, will be 'reversing' items. In other words, what is a reconciling item one month will be cleared the next.

Other items, such as mixing private and business money, will be permanent and you should record these as you go along.

Most reconciliation problems can be dealt with by applying a little logic and if you get into the routine of reconciling your bank account every month you will learn how to deal with the occasional oddity or missed transaction.

If you struggle to complete your bank reconciliation don't be afraid to get some help. Bank reconciliations are probably the most troublesome problem people face with basic bookkeeping, but are certainly worth doing as they help ensure your records are accurate.

Check Totals

Check totals can be used to make sure all the individual expense columns add up correctly.

In the example expenses layout in Figure 2.3, the total of the 'Amount' column should be the same as the total of all the individual analysis columns. In other words, the total of the 'Stationery' column (£59.50) plus 'Books' (£24.95) plus Drawings (£105) equals the total of the 'Amount' column £189.45.

Spreadsheet Tip

You can use a check formula to add up the sum of all the analysis columns and check this is the same as the total of the 'Amount' column. If you put this formula just under the total of the Amount column (see Figure 2.5) it will alert you where there is a difference.

Figure 2.5 Looking for Counting Errors

	A	B	C	D	E	F	G	H
1								
2	No.	Date	Payee	Description	Amount	Stationery	Books	Drawings
3								
4	1	05/01/2018	Staples	Office Supplies	59.50	59.50		
5	2	06/01/2018	Taxcafe	Books	24.95		24.95	
6	3	22/01/2018	Self	Drawings	105.00			105.00
7								
8					189.45	59.50	24.95	105.00
9								
10					0			
11								

In this example the spreadsheet formula would be:

=sum(E4:E6) – sum(F8:H8)

If the number in the box is not zero you can immediately see something is wrong with your analysis.

If you're using manual books you will have to manually add up the column totals and check this comes back to the total of the 'Amount'. Typically you would do that at the bottom of each page as you go on through your accounts book.

Chapter 3

How to Send Out Invoices That Get Paid!

A common question from owners of new businesses is: "How do I lay out an invoice?" I have put together some examples for both a simple sole trader and a VAT-registered limited company – the latter is discussed more fully in later sections of this book.

Do I Need an Invoice?

Not all businesses issue invoices. If you deal in retail where the customer buys goods 'over the counter' using cash or a credit card, you normally just issue a till receipt. Similarly, many online businesses that deal only with consumer items don't give out invoices.

Principally you need to provide an invoice if:

- You get paid *after* you supply the goods or services.
- You are dealing with other businesses and they require a proper invoice to be raised.

What Should I Include on My Invoice?

Your invoice should contain the same details as your headed paper. The details for headed paper are set out in Appendix 1.

In addition, you must include the following information:

- The word 'Invoice'
- The date of the invoice

A basic invoice for a non-VAT-registered service company may look similar to the example one in Figure 3.1.

Figure 3.1 A Sample Invoice

Company Name			Address Line 1
			Address Line 2
LOGO			Address Line 3
		Telephone	01234 567890

Billing Address			
Mr A		**Invoice**	
Address Line 1			
Address Line 2		Invoice Ref	INV001
Address Line 3		Invoice Date	05/01/2018
Address Line 4			

Qty	Description		Total (£)
2	Weasels		£ 800.00
1	Badger		£ 200.00
		Total	£ 1,000.00

You must include your name and address and that of the customer, the invoice number, date and a list of the items sold.

If you are selling lots of multiple items you may like to have an additional column showing the price per item and the quantity of each item.

More Complex Invoices

If you are VAT-registered you need to include the following additional information:

- The VAT element of the invoice should be clearly stated.
- VAT rate 20%.
- The date of supply or 'tax point' (this is explored in more detail in the VAT section below).

I also strongly suggest you include the following so that customers can pay you easily:

- Payment terms (14 days, 30 days etc).
- Due date of the invoice.
- Payment instructions, i.e. the name of the person/company to whom any cheques are payable, plus your bank account details for direct payments plus any reference details required.
- Contact name and number for any queries.

These bits of information are included to help your customers pay you as quickly as possible. I don't know about you, but I'm always put off paying an invoice if I first have to ring up to ask the bank account details or to whom my cheque should be made payable

Most businesses now make all their payments via electronic or internet banking, so not including your details seems rather amateurish, not to mention rather damaging to your cash flow if you are put to the bottom of the pile.

The same invoice for a VAT-registered business would look something like Figure 3.2. I have incorporated the additional payment information in a box at the bottom.

Spreadsheet Tip

If you are using spreadsheet software to generate your invoices, it is straightforward to enter one date as the 'invoice date' and let the 'due date' and 'tax point' be calculated automatically with a simple formula. Similarly, you should be able to get your spreadsheet to work out the VAT for you automatically once you have entered the line totals.

Figure 3.2 Sample Invoice – VAT Included

Company Name		Address Line 1
		Address Line 2
LOGO		Address Line 3
	Telephone	01234 567890

Billing Address

Mr A
Address Line 1

Invoice

Address Line 2	Invoice Ref	INV001
Address Line 3	Invoice Date	05/01/2018
Address Line 4	Tax Point	05/01/2018
	Terms	14 Days
	DUE DATE	**19/01/2018**

Qty	Description		Total (£)	
2	Weasels		£	800.00
1	Badger		£	200.00
		Sub Total	£	1,000.00
		Vat @ 20%	£	200.00
		TOTAL	£	**1,200.00**

Payment Details

This invoice is **due for payment by the 19th January 2018**
Payment should be made to Bank Name account no. 12345678, sort code 00-00-00
Cheques should be made payable to "Company Name" and sent to the above address

Company Trading Name is the trading name of Company Legal Name Ltd
Registered in England No. 01234567. VAT registration number 123456789

From a VAT point of view we can see the addition of the tax point (normally the same as the invoice date) and the VAT amounts clearly listed.

If some of the items you are selling are subject to VAT and others are not, you will either have to issue separate invoices for the different items or add two new columns for 'VAT' and 'Gross' so that the VAT element on each item is clearly shown. This won't apply to most readers.

From a credit control point of view we can see the payment details listed quite prominently with the due date in the payment details box. This should help with this document's main purpose – getting your business paid for the goods or services provided.

By now you should have a good idea what to include on your invoices. It's worth looking at the invoices other people send you and thinking about what works and what doesn't in the context of your business. For example, if everyone pays you before you dispatch goods, then there is very little point including the payment instructions section that is crucial to many service businesses.

Chapter 4

What Records the Taxman Expects You to Keep

Why Keep Records?

To take your record keeping to the next level it helps to think about *why* you need to keep records. There are two principal reasons:

- To prepare your self-assessment tax return.
- For management purposes – in other words, to help you improve your business.

Preparing the self-assessment return is probably what most sole traders are concerned about but creating your own management accounts, with which you can measure the performance of your business and identify any problems, is just as important.

Successful businesses tend to integrate their accounting systems and their operational ones. This may sound complicated but it can be as simple as using the same spreadsheet to record income for accounts purposes as you do for recording which of your invoices remain unpaid.

By having one set of documents that are central to your business you can reduce the chances of errors or omissions. If your record keeping is an afterthought it will tend to result in problems in the longer term.

As a small sole trader the requirements for record keeping are not nearly as onerous as for a limited company or larger enterprise. This section details the types of information you will need to record and retain so that you can complete your self assessment tax return at the end of the year.

There are three basic classes of information you need to record.

Class of Information	Basic Requirements
Sales	Total sales income received. Evidence of completeness of sales.
Expenses	All business expenses by statutory category with supporting invoices as evidence.
Stock	Value of opening and closing stocks on hand.

Sales

The basic record-keeping procedure described in Chapter 1 will generally be sufficient for most small businesses. As you will recall, this simply involves listing all invoices you have sent out, backed up by the invoices themselves or the invoice book.

You should also record any invoices that remain unpaid at the year-end, especially if you do not expect to receive any payment.

Some businesses do not send invoices if they deal mainly with cash or earn commissions. In this instance retain the till rolls or commission statements as evidence of your income.

You may prefer to group daily or weekly payments rather than list a large number of small items. This is perfectly acceptable, provided you have the full information available for inspection by the taxman.

If you have a cash business, the completeness of your records may well be questioned. Ideally, bank your takings daily or weekly so the money can be seen arriving in your business bank account. This will be helpful in the long run, especially if you can show all payments received are traceable through the bank account.

Expenses

If your business has a turnover of less than £85,000 you can if you wish report your expenses as a single lump sum on your tax return. You are not required to split them up into different categories. Businesses with a turnover in excess £85,000 are required to split their expenses up into certain 'statutory' categories.

HMRC guidance detailing what expenses to include in each category is contained in Appendix 2. The categories include:

- Costs of goods bought for re-sale
- Construction industry – payments to subcontractors
- Wages, salaries and other staff costs
- Car, van and travel expenses
- Rent, rates, power and insurance costs
- Repair and renewals of property and equipment
- Telephone, fax, stationery and other office costs
- Advertising and business entertainment
- Interest on bank and other loans
- Bank, credit card and other financial charges
- Irrecoverable debts written off
- Accountancy, legal and other professional fees
- Depreciation and loss/profit on sale of assets
- Other business expenses

Earlier we saw how expenses could be put into different categories. In choosing which categories to use you should try to ensure you don't put together expenses that need to be shown separately on your tax return.

For example, you might quite reasonably have a category called 'Office' and record all your office expenses within this category, including paying the office rent and insurance. At year-end you will find 'Rent, rates and power and insurance' and 'Telephone, fax stationery and other office costs' are *separate* categories. You will then have to go back and split up a year's worth of transactions.

Problems like this are easy to avoid with a bit of forward planning. Simply split up your expenses into the relevant statutory categories and you'll keep the taxman happy! It's probably worth having a look through the categories now to see which ones apply to your business.

Some sole traders set up their accounts using only the statutory categories. However, as we will see below, it can be a good idea, from a management information perspective, to have subcategories.

You may wish to analyse 'Telephone', 'Website Costs', 'Stationery' and 'Other Office Expenses', all of which are reported on your tax return under the single statutory category: 'Telephone, fax, stationery and other office costs'.

There's a potentially big difference between 'management accounting' and 'financial accounting'. Management accounting is all about using accounting information to help you run your business more efficiently and make it more profitable. This type of information is often kept confidential so that competitors do not get their hands on it.

Financial accounting, on the other hand, is all about complying with rules and regulations: completing your tax return and producing annual accounts if your business is run through a limited company.

Stock

If your business has stock (in other words, if it sells goods rather than services) you must keep a record of the stock on hand at the end of the financial year. A simple stock count will normally suffice. If you have large volumes of low-value items, estimates are permitted based on, for example, weight or physical volume.

Note that stock is valued at cost rather than sales price.

Checklist of Records to Keep

The following is a checklist of the information you need to retain for proper accounting records. You need to keep this information for up to six years:

- Purchase receipts or other evidence of purchases
- Sales invoices or other evidence of income
- Closing stock records at year end
- Company bank statements
- Paying-in books and cheque book stubs
- Your summary accounting records

Don't be tempted to throw these things out if your business closes. A few boxes at the back of your garage may well save you a lot of problems if you are ever subject to an HMRC investigation.

It is perfectly acceptable to keep all of this data electronically but, if you do, make sure it is:

(a) A complete record, not just some of the data
(b) Within your direct control to access
(c) Properly backed up

There is nothing more painful for a client under a tax investigation whose 'electronic records' consist of some incomplete data on a long since broken laptop, a smattering of purchase invoices which may or may not be attached to some old emails, and the wrongful assumption that an ex-supplier will allow indefinite access to old purchase invoices on an online portal. Don't let this be you!

Registering as a Sole Trader or Partnership

You are asked to register your sole trader business (or partnership) "as soon as you can". In practice, as long as you don't miss any filing deadlines there won't be a penalty.

Registration puts you in the self-assessment tax system, so you will automatically receive a tax return and reminders.

The following page on HMRC's website deals with registration:

https://www.gov.uk/set-up-sole-trader

At the time of writing there were two basic choices: you can use the online form CWF1, or you can fill in a different on-screen form which you can print and post to HMRC. Here's the link to the online form:

https://www.tax.service.gov.uk/shortforms/form/CWF1ST

The online form is good if you already have a 10 digit UTR number due to having filled in a tax return in the past (clue: it will be on the top of most correspondence from HMRC, such as an old tax return, or a payment reminder).

If this is your first time dealing with tax returns, you will also need to set up a Government Gateway account and apply for a UTR number before you can use form CWF1 which will take a couple of weeks to show up in the post.

Due to the delay waiting for a UTR number, you may find it neater to use the on-screen postal form because this lets you do the whole thing in one go. You will find the link to the on-screen form under "Other ways to register" on this page:

gov.uk/log-in-file-self-assessment-tax-return/register-if-youre-self-employed

Tip: I would generally suggest you wait until you know you have a working business before registering for self-assessment. If you are keen and register in the "planning" phase of a new business, you will end up being sent a tax return by HMRC regardless of whether your business actually takes off. For accounting periods commencing April 2017, if your turnover *(not profit)* is less than £1,000 you won't need to declare your income in any case.

Where to Go From Here

This first section should have helped you appreciate some of the basic bookkeeping requirements of a small sole trader business. For many readers, especially those just starting out in business, this should be more than sufficient for now.

Others may be feeling a bit shell-shocked and in need of a good cup of tea! If this is you, it may help to put this book away and read it again tomorrow, perhaps using your own information to go through the Basic Bookkeeping section before reading further.

Don't be too disheartened if you still aren't happy with your records. This section is not exhaustive and will not suit everyone's methods of learning and business situation and, quite frankly, not everyone wants to do their own bookkeeping.

Suggested Next Steps

- Re-read this section at least once.

- Try to identify what <u>your</u> reporting needs are.

- Jot down the types of expenses you have and the ones you want to keep an eye on.

- Set out a basic structure for your accounts, along the lines discussed above.

- Put your receipts and income in a logical order (probably date order).

- Start filling in your records, for example using a spreadsheet listing all your expenses.

- Adjust your record structure as your needs change. Your first ideas will probably need to be refined a number of times during the first 12 months as the business develops.

- When you receive your bank statement, remember to reconcile it. Don't try to do more than one month at a time – the more transactions; the harder it is to perform.

Section 2

Introducing VAT

Chapter 5

How VAT Works in Plain English

If VAT is new to you, read on! This chapter will help you understand the basics, even if you don't intend to register right now.

Businesses are not automatically VAT registered so if you haven't applied for and obtained a VAT number you won't be currently registered for VAT.

Chapter 25, "Who Should Register for VAT Early?" explores in more detail whether voluntary registration is suitable for your business and how to go about it. Registration is compulsory if your turnover exceeds the VAT threshold. The threshold has been frozen at £85,000 until 31st March 2020 while the Government consults on various issues surrounding VAT registration.

So what exactly is VAT?

- Value Added Tax (VAT) is charged on the supply of most good and services.

- The standard VAT rate is 20%.

- Only VAT-registered companies charge VAT on their sales.

- Only VAT-registered companies can reclaim VAT on their costs.

- VAT-registered companies administer and collect VAT on behalf of HM Revenue and Customs, the government body responsible for VAT.

20% of What Exactly?

The quoted rate of 20% is applied to the net value of an invoice. So if a VAT-registered company wants to receive a net price of £100 it will add a further 20% VAT and sell the item at £120.

Example

Net value of invoice	*£100.00*
VAT at 20%	*£ 20.00*
Gross value of invoice	*£120.00*

If the company wishes to sell at a total price of £100 the net selling price is found by dividing the gross price by 1.2.

For example:

Gross value of invoice	*£100.00*
Net value of the invoice (£100/1.2)	*£ 83.33*
Vat (£83.33 multiplied by 20%)	*£ 16.67*

Taxcafe's free VAT calculator lets you perform calculations such as these at the touch of a button. It is available at:

www.taxcafe.co.uk/vatcalc

Now we can calculate VAT, it is helpful to see how it works in practice.

Example

Tom chops down trees for a living and is VAT registered.

Tom sells £1,000 of wood to Dick and gives him an invoice for £1,200 (£1,000 plus £200 VAT).

Dick pays Tom the total amount of £1,200. Tom keeps £1,000 and pays £200 to HMRC when he submits his VAT return.

Dick is a furniture maker and also VAT registered. He takes the £1,000 worth of wood and makes a table for Harry. Harry is the end consumer and has agreed to pay a total of £3,600 for the table.

Dick gets his calculator out and works out that if Harry is prepared to pay £3,600 in total, he must charge him £3,000 plus VAT of £600.

Appearing on Dick's VAT return will be £600 of 'output tax' (the VAT on his sales). This money has to be paid to HMRC.

Dick also has £200 'input tax' (the VAT on the wood he bought from Tom). This money has to be <u>claimed back</u> from HMRC.

The difference between his output tax and his input tax – £400 – is the actual amount paid over to the VAT man.

On Dick's income tax return he will ignore VAT and declare net sales of £3,000 and net purchases of £1,000, resulting in a profit of £2,000.

The VAT man has received £200 from Tom and £400 from Dick. This is the same as the total VAT of £600 paid by Harry. However, Harry doesn't pay the VAT man directly – instead Tom and Dick effectively take on the role of tax collectors.

In other businesses the same principles apply – VAT-registered companies collect VAT and pass it on to HMRC.

Who Really Ends Up Paying the Tax?

If a business is VAT registered it can claim back all the tax it has paid on its expenses, so there is no real financial loss.

But if your business is not VAT registered you cannot claim back any VAT you pay so there is a real financial loss. Everything you buy from VAT-registered businesses will cost 20% more.

What about your income and sales – who really pays the VAT on the invoices you send out? If you send a VAT invoice to a VAT-registered business, that business doesn't care because it knows it can reclaim that VAT.

But if you send an invoice to a business that is not registered, or if your customer is a private individual, the VAT represents a real added cost because the tax cannot be recovered by the customer.

The critical question now is who really pays the tax: your business or your customer?

If you were able to sell 100 widgets for £100 before you were VAT registered and can still sell 100 widgets for £100 + £20 VAT after registering, then it is your customer who is absorbing the VAT – you have managed to pass the entire VAT cost onto them.

However, if after registering for VAT you can only sell 100 widgets for £83.33 + £16.67 VAT then it is your business that is worse off – you have not managed to pass on any of the VAT cost to your customers, and have a much lower net income (£83.33 as opposed to £100). This might happen if there are competitors out there who are not VAT registered and can still sell 100 widgets for £100. This can be quite a common issue for small businesses.

Chapter 6

VAT Jargon Demystified

It is important to get to grips with the following basic VAT terminology:

Inputs	The value of the goods and services <u>received or purchased</u> by your business, i.e. goods in.
Input VAT	The value of the VAT on the inputs
Outputs	The value of the goods or services <u>supplied or sold</u> by your business, i.e. goods out.
Output VAT	The value of the VAT on the outputs

Non-standard VAT Rates

No doubt you have come across invoices that don't have any VAT on them or the VAT is at a reduced rate (for example, the VAT rate on domestic electricity bills is 5%). This may be because the business that sends out the invoice is either VAT exempt or sells 'zero-rated' products.

VAT-exempt Firms

Some firms do not have to add VAT to their invoices. This may be because they are under the VAT registration threshold or because they supply services that are VAT exempt. For example, banks do not levy VAT on many of their charges.

Although they don't need to charge VAT, exempt firms cannot reclaim VAT on their purchases, so it isn't always a great position to be in.

Zero-rated Firms

Zero-rated firms are those that don't have to charge any VAT on their sales but can reclaim the VAT paid on expenses. As it happens, these firms do theoretically charge VAT on their sales but at the rate of 0%! This means they are permanently receiving VAT refunds for the tax paid on their expenses.

Zero-rated businesses include food sellers (but not restaurant meals or hot takeaways), bookshops and publishers of printed books, suppliers of children's clothing and shoes and exporters.

If you do sell zero-rated items it makes sense to register for VAT so that you can reclaim all the VAT on your expenses without having to charge any VAT to your customers.

VAT on Imports and Exports of Goods

Non-registered Businesses

If you are not VAT registered and purchase goods from other EU countries, you will simply pay any VAT (or the equivalent EU tax) added to your purchases.

If you buy goods from outside the EU, UK VAT will be added and you may also have to pay import duty.

VAT-registered Businesses

If your business is VAT registered you can buy goods from companies in Europe free of VAT (or the equivalent EU tax) by providing the company with your VAT number before the invoice is issued. You cannot reclaim overseas VAT when you submit your UK VAT return. Similarly, your sales to VAT registered customers in European countries can be zero rated (providing you obtain your customers' VAT details).

If you make purchases outside the EU these will be subject to UK VAT but this can be reclaimed when you submit your VAT return. You may also have to pay import duty and other import costs which can mount up, so remember to do your research before placing any overseas orders.

Import & Export Tips

- When selling in the EU and charging no VAT, quote the purchaser's VAT number on your invoice to prove you have obtained it.

- You can't directly reclaim EU VAT on your normal VAT return, but you can make a reclaim of some EU VAT through a reclaim system hosted by HMRC:

  www.gov.uk/vat-refunds-for-uk-businesses-buying-from-other-eu-countries

  This may be worthwhile if you, for example, travel frequently to Europe on business, but the rules do vary considerably.

  For example, if you happen to be at a conference in one country you may be able to reclaim VAT on your hotel, meals and conference tickets.

  In another country you may only be able to reclaim the VAT on your conference ticket, and in another the VAT on your accommodation may be reclaimed but you won't get any VAT back on your meals.

  Individual circumstances need to be looked at carefully to determine if a claim is worthwhile. Whilst HMRC does provide much of the infrastructure, you will still end up dealing with each country you are claiming from in turn.

  If this sounds too complex to deal with yourself, you can find a selection of companies offering a dedicated VAT reclaim service by going to a search engine like Google and typing "EU VAT Reclaim".

Summary Table

	Imports (Goods Purchases)	Export (Goods Sales)
EU – Your Business Not Registered	Overseas VAT added to your purchases.	No VAT.
EU – Your Business VAT Registered	Provide your VAT number to your supplier to be invoiced with no European VAT.	You must include VAT on your sales unless the purchaser provides you with a European VAT number. You may then invoice without any VAT.
World	VAT added by Customs to physical imports.	No VAT chargeable on your invoice. Local taxes may apply in the export country.

VAT on Imports and Exports of Services

If you are a VAT registered company providing services to other EU countries or worldwide, there is an extra complication known as the 'place of supply' rules.

These rules are complex but broadly what they aim to do is levy VAT, not where the end customer is, but where the business 'belongs', in other words where the service is actually performed.

This means that if you are a service business you may still have to charge UK VAT for services provided to customers outside the UK, especially if you are selling to consumers and not business clients.

There are an awful lot of specific rules in this area, principally concerning land, transport and broadcast media, but also covering a large number of other areas, including digitally delivered services which have their own special rules as discussed in the next section.

Example 1

Claire provides proof-reading services for scientific papers for academics. Her customers are based in the UK, US and in Poland. The place of supply for a consumer is where the work is performed, that is to say the UK. Claire must therefore charge UK VAT to her non-VAT registered Polish customers. Under the general place of supply rules she notes she ought to also charge VAT to her US customers, but as her service is included on a list of services where the place of supply CAN be considered the customer's home for non-EU customers, she can avoid charging VAT to her US customers. Phew!

This rather tortuous explanation is how the rules are written: "you must do this unless", which makes reading the guidance particularly difficult. If you deal with items that are physically present in other countries it is even possible to end up paying overseas VAT.

Example 2

Claire decides to organise a large scientific conference in Poland and receives money from ticket sales in both the UK and Poland. As the place of supply is deemed to be the location of the conference, and not where her business 'belongs', she is somewhat surprised to find a Polish VAT officer demanding that she pays over Polish VAT on the ticket sales!

For more details on this topic please see the HMRC website:

www.gov.uk/vat-how-to-work-out-your-place-of-supply-of-services

The detail can be found in Notice 741A, which is linked to in the above webpage but can also be easily found by typing "VAT Notice 741A" into Google. Do however be careful as there is also a Notice 741 which only applies to January 2010.

I should point out that, as a general accountant rather than a VAT specialist, even I have to take advice on this topic from time to time and I would suggest that you do the same if necessary.

VAT and Digitally Delivered Services

There are special VAT rules which apply to businesses supplying "digital services" to consumers within the EU. This could be software such as a mobile phone app or computer game, or something less obvious such as an e-book sold on your website.

From January 2019 this only applies if your turnover to the EU exceeds €10,000. The bad news is that at the time of writing there was no minimum limit in place.

The rules seek to "level the playing field" by ensuring that, no matter where the supplier is, the customer is charged the local VAT rate. So if you are based in the UK you will be charging local rates of VAT to customers in France, even though France's VAT rate may be different to that in the UK. The aim is to stop firms relocating within the EU, or even outside the EU, to avoid or reduce the VAT they charge.

This sounds quite sensible until you realise that, as a retailer of digital products across the EU, you will need to charge different rates of VAT to different customers.

Faced with what would otherwise be a herculean task of registering for VAT in every EU country, the European VAT authorities have come up with a fairly decent system called the "Mini One Stop Shop" (MOSS). This allows you to pay over EU VAT in one place, with one form and one payment. This is due once a quarter:

www.gov.uk/register-and-use-the-vat-mini-one-stop-shop

So far so good but there are two key areas that have caused considerable angst amongst small businesses:

1. The legislation can apply to ALL businesses, not just those over the UK VAT threshold, or indeed those registered for VAT.

2. There is until January 2019 no minimum reporting threshold. In theory even a one-off £5 e-book sale to Italy means you need to register for MOSS and fill in the form.

Initial feedback from HMRC during 2015 was that they are not much interested in small traders 'clogging up' the system and actively invited over 3,000 'hobby businesses' to leave MOSS.

The problem we have in 2018 is that the €10,000 rule isn't law yet, and whilst there doesn't seem to be any enforcement at a low level, that isn't to say there won't be. We know from the relatively low number of registrations that many traders are taking a risk and ignoring the whole issue on the basis that they are too small to pursue.

However, you could in theory face local fines in *each and every country* in which you fail to operate properly. As I don't have detailed knowledge of VAT rules in each EU country I can't tell you what those fines might be and there's no guarantee the penalties would be limited to VAT due.

All of this leaves businesses in a frustrating position. Complying with the law as it stands will take up a disproportionate amount of time; failure to comply could result in substantial fines and penalties.

For those who need to operate MOSS here are a few practical tips:

- Synchronise your normal VAT 'stagger' dates to the MOSS dates which are March/June/September/December. This means you can file your main VAT return at the same time.

- Some of the larger e-commerce platforms will take care of the VAT for you and pay you the net "after VAT" income. This is helpful for small volume sales.

- When selling to consumers there is no need to split out the VAT at the point of sale unless asked to do so. Therefore you can simply charge everyone the same end sales price, and work out the VAT later.

- If EU sales volumes are low, consider just blocking them from your website entirely. If the cost of compliance is higher than the income generated there is no point making these sales at all.

Section 3

How Good Accounts Help a Business Grow

Chapter 7

Introduction

This section develops the themes from the Basic Bookkeeping section. If you've jumped straight in here, you may find it worthwhile flicking through the previous sections to ensure you have not missed anything.

Obviously I can't cover all eventualities and business types in a guide such as this. For example, for a business that earns all its income from large companies and is paid three months after invoice date, credit control and cash flow are going to be very important.

Credit control is not an issue where all income is received before delivery. To get most benefit from reading this book you need to think about your own specific business needs.

To help you do this we'll take a look at two case studies in the next two chapters, the first involving James who sells e-books online, the second involving Emily who sells works of art.

James sells his e-books on his own website and on E-bay. He has a large number of small sales that are paid for in advance using PayPal, the well-known online payment company.

Emily sells a small number of art works purchased from third parties. She holds some items in stock and clients pay her by cheque.

Their management accounting needs are somewhat more involved than their needs for tax purposes and each will require different information.

Chapter 8

Case Study 1: James's Bookshop

The following table (Figure 8.1) summarises James's basic accounting information requirements:

Figure 8.1 Why James Needs Accounts

For Tax Purposes	For Management Purposes
• Total sales in the year	• Sales by time period (week/month) • Sales by book title
• Total expenses in the year with supporting evidence	• Expense totals by type

Sales

James wants to know how much he makes in total each week from selling e-books, which titles are selling and which are not. He'd also like to know where the books are sold (on his website or on eBay). He doesn't really want a detailed list of all sales, as that would be too much information.

James doesn't send out invoices so the first question is, where does he source his accounting information? We know all sales (both from his website and from Ebay) are processed by PayPal, the online credit card payment processor. So this seems the logical place to start.

From PayPal he can obtain a weekly summary that lists the income and credit card processing charges between given dates. He could print this out every week and enter the information on a spreadsheet, like the one in Figure 8.2

Figure 8.2 James's Sales

Week	Description	Amount	Book 1	Book 2	Book 3
01/01/2018	eBay	1,000.00	250.00	150.00	600.00
08/01/2018	eBay	250.00	150.00	50.00	50.00
08/01/2018	Website	100.00	25.00	25.00	50.00
Total		**1,350.00**	**425.00**	**225.00**	**700.00**

- 'Week' now gives the week in which the sales occurred, rather than invoice numbers.
- 'Description' states the source of the income.
- 'Amount' shows the weekly sales income received.
- 'Book 1', 'Book 2', 'Book 3' show the sales of each of James's books.

These new analysis columns allow James to see which titles are doing well. Alternatively he may wish to record the number of sales instead of the value.

What works for your business only you can decide but it isn't hard to build extra 'management' information like this into your accounting records.

We can see that in the week starting January 8th James received some sales directly from his website and some from eBay. He has chosen to put two lines on the spreadsheet for January 8th to distinguish where his sales have come from.

This is where having the extra descriptive field comes in handy and using a basic spreadsheet set up more fields can be entered or removed as required.

From this very basic arrangement James can find out:

- In which week sales occurred
- Which titles are selling
- The source of the sale

It wouldn't take a lot of work to analyse this data in lots of different ways to help James spot trends and therefore improve the running of his business.

Expenses

James wants to know how much he is spending on eBay auction fees, PayPal credit card charges and general office expenditure. He uses the same basic layout that we used in Figure 2.3 earlier, with the revised headings as follows:

Figure 8.3 James's Expenses

No.	Date	Payee	Description	Amount	Stationery	Paypal	eBay
1	05/01/2018	Staples	Office Supplies	59.50	59.50		
2	06/01/2018	Paypal	Transaction Fees	8.99		8.99	
3	08/01/2018	eBay	Sellers Fees	105.00			105.00
4	09/01/2018	PayPal	Transaction Fees	8.50		8.50	
				181.99	59.50	17.49	105.00

Specific Points about eBay and PayPal Fees

For accounting purposes we need to show both the gross income (in other words, the total turnover before fees) and the full eBay and PayPal fees that have been charged.

For example, James may sell a book for £10 but only receive £9.00 in his PayPal account. Sales income would be shown as £10 gross and PayPal expenses of £1.00.

This can be a bit disconcerting at first, as you are creating two transactions from one amount, but you need to think about what has actually happened.

- James has sold an item at the full price of £10
- PayPal has charged him a merchant fee of £1

Had the merchant fee been charged at the end of the month you would be able to see the two underlying transactions clearly – an income and an expense.

The confusing thing about PayPal and other online transactions is that both transactions occur at the same time. You are in receipt of the net amount, rather than receiving the full sales income and then paying the charge at a later date.

Recognition of Sales

From a management point of view, James would like to show in his accounts when sales are *earned*. That is to say, when he makes a sale rather than when the cash is physically transferred into his business bank account.

If money is transferred from his PayPal account to his bank account on a weekly basis then treating the sales as having occurred on the date of transfer to his bank account would seem a pragmatic approach.

If, however, he uses his PayPal account for storing funds and perhaps for paying for other purchases, he may need to treat his PayPal account as he would any other business bank account and carry out reconciliations.

> **Tip:** When a business uses PayPal for receiving sales income, be strict and ONLY use the account for income. This makes life simple from an accounts point of view as there are no "hidden" expenses and you can simply add up the transfers into the business bank account rather than dig through all the transactions.

Taxable Transactions

There is unfortunately a lot of uninformed comment in the press about what is and isn't taxable when it comes to selling things on eBay.

The tax rules for eBay sales are the same as for any other business. If you are involved in a 'trade'– in other words if you buy and sell for a profit motive – then you are deemed to be 'trading' and your profits are taxable.

If you sell a few items that you originally purchased for your own use or were, say, given for Christmas, this is not trading and not taxable.

Chapter 9

Case Study 2: Emily's Art

Emily's business is more complex than James's. She buys and sells stock items (paintings) and is paid by cheque. Each customer is sent an invoice and only pays after this has been received. Figure 9.1 summarises Emily's basic information requirements.

Figure 9.1 Why Emily Needs Accounts

For Tax Purposes	For Management Purposes
• Total sales in the year	• Sales by time (week/month) • Sales by client • Profit per picture • Debtors – who owes money
• Expenses by statutory category with supporting evidence	• Expense totals by type of spend
• Stock on hand at year end	• Stock on hand by picture

Sales

Emily's two key management tasks are:

- Stock control (knowing how much stock should be held and how much should be ordered), and

- Ensuring each invoice is paid.

These tasks should determine how Emily designs her accounting records.

The sales spreadsheet may look something like Figure 9.2:

Figure 9.2 Emily's Sales

Ref	Invoice Date	Customer	Artist	Amount	Paid Date	Cost	Gross Profit
INV001	01/01/2018	Mr A	Anna	1,000.00	08/01/2017	700.00	300.00
INV002	02/01/2018	Mr C	Paul	250.00	22/01/2017	100.00	150.00
INV003	05/01/2018	Mrs D	Peter	100.00		25.00	75.00
Total				1,350.00		825.00	525.00

- 'Ref' - the invoice reference.
- 'Invoice date' - the date of the sale.
- 'Customer' - who has bought the picture.
- 'Artist' - which artist painted the piece.
- 'Amount' - the amount invoiced.

There are also some extra descriptive fields:

- 'Paid Date' shows the date the invoice was paid. This column is very useful to track whose payments are outstanding and help with the bank reconciliation. Using this column Emily can see quickly who still owes her for the paintings and take appropriate credit control action. For Emily this is very important. As we can see, Mrs D has not yet paid for the painting sent on January 5th and needs to be chased up.

- The 'Cost' and 'Gross Profit' columns are useful because they show how much has been made on each picture. Gross profit is simply sales minus costs of goods sold, so if Emily buys a picture for £100 and sells it for £250 her gross profit is £150. Gross profit does not take account of operating expenses such as stationery, telephone and office rent.

  If Emily had a large number of paintings, each at a standard mark-up, the gross profit number would be superfluous. Because she has a small number of items at varying mark-ups she can quickly see what her gross profits are for the period.

You could of course add extra fields to suit your needs, for example Emily could add the name of the piece of art or a list of paintings ordered but not yet invoiced.

The aim of management accounts is to allow *you* to run your business successfully and keep the paperwork to a minimum.

Expenses

Emily's requirements for recording expenses are no different to James's apart from the category titles, so I won't elaborate on this point.

Stock

Stock management is crucial to Emily's business so suitable records must be kept. There are many ways of doing this but a simple list such as the one in Figure 9.3 will suffice:

Figure 9.3 Emily's Stock Management

Date Purchased	Artist	Item Name	Purchase Price	Date Sold		Stock Value
01/12/2017	Anna	Flowers	700.00	01/01/2018		-
01/12/2017	Paul	Seascape	100.00	02/01/2018		-
01/12/2017	Peter	Calm	25.00	05/01/2018		-
01/12/2017	John	Face	400.00	Stock		400.00
	Total		1,225.00			400.00

The above spreadsheet contains the purchase date and purchase price, the date the item was sold and some descriptive columns for the supplier (the artist in this case) and item name (the name of the painting).

The Stock Value column can be linked to the Purchase Price column using a simple formula. For example, if the purchase price of the Face painting is stored in cell D7 of the spreadsheet, Emily could type '=D7' in the Stock Value column. The number '400' will then appear as it does above. Then, when the Face painting is sold, she could simply replace the number 400 with a '0' or '-'. This way there is always a 'live' stock value.

By including the 'Date Sold' column it is always possible to go back and establish the stock level at an earlier date, if required for accounting purposes. It may also be possible to combine both the sales and stock pages on one sheet, although this could become a bit cumbersome. If Emily was dealing with a large volume of similar items (for example, say she bought 5,000 postcards to sell) a different approach would be needed.

There are many ways of doing this. Figure 9.4 suggests a typical layout for a stock record with large volumes of identical items:

Figure 9.4 Stock Management – Large Volumes

Date	Description	Amount	Sales	Quantity	1	2	3
		£	£				
01/01/2018	Purchase - A	200.00	-	5,000	2,400	1,500	1,100
07/01/2018	Sales		(34.76)	(869)	(124)	(325)	(420)
14/01/2018	Sales		(11.28)	(282)	(27)	(25)	(230)
Total		200.00	(46.04)	3,849	2,249	1,150	450

- 'Date' gives the date of the transaction.
- 'Description' gives the type of transaction, either a purchase of stock or a sale.
- 'Amount' gives the amount paid for the stock.
- 'Sales' is the *cost of goods sold*, based on an average unit cost of 4p per unit (5,000 cards bought for £200). In this example 4p is the known cost of the stock.
- 'Quantity' is the physical quantity of cards purchased or sold.
- '1, 2, 3' give the stock levels of each design.

Using this approach you can quickly see the level of each stock item without manually checking your stock levels. You also have some idea of the level of transactions to enable you to plan your stock replenishment.

Again real-life examples may be more or less complex than this example and if you deal with a lot of stock you may find upgrading to a proper accounting system is preferable.

This is particularly useful if you have a large range of items with different prices and mark-ups that is too complex for a simple spreadsheet.

If you're a small trader, setting out your accounts as described above will give you a basic structure to get you started. You can then build and adapt this as your business needs dictate.

Section 4

How to Complete Your Tax Return Without Fuss

Chapter 10

Business Tax Return Basics

In this section I will show you how to prepare the self employment pages of your tax return.

This is by no means an exhaustive explanation and is designed to show you how the accounting information discussed above fits into your return.

Even if you have no intention of completing your tax return yourself and would prefer an accountant to do it for you, it's well worth reading this section so that you understand where the numbers you produce for your business end up and why certain things in your accounts are important.

Know your Dates

The first thing you need to know is the date your return has to be completed.

- The tax year runs from 6 April to 5 April the following year.
- The tax year ending on 5 April 2018 is denoted 2017/18.
- Payments for the period to 5 April 2018 have to be made by 31 January 2019.
- Paper tax returns for 2017/18 should be submitted by 31 October 2018.
- Online returns for 2017/18 have to be submitted by 31 January 2019.

Remember, however long you've got, it's never too early to make a start on your tax return.

The longer you leave it, the less chance you have of getting help from either an accountant or HMRC. Furthermore, returns completed at the last minute are more likely to lead to higher tax bills, given the tendency of most people to err on the side of caution.

Tip: Early filing will give you earlier conclusion of your affairs. HMRC must open an enquiry into your return within 12 months of the date of your having submitted it, the 'enquiry window', so the sooner you file the sooner you will have certainty of your affairs.

Tip: The online filing system doesn't always cope too well with the 31st January rush, so you will avoid a lot of frustration if you start to think about completing your self assessment return when you are still mowing the grass rather than whilst taking down the Christmas decorations.

The penalty system for the late filing of tax returns is quite harsh. There is a minimum penalty of £100 for missing the deadlines, regardless of the amount of tax due. The penalties are based on a combination of how late the return is, how late the payment of tax is, and the amount of tax arising.

Someone who is, for example, 12 months late filing their 2018 return will face a minimum penalty of £1,600 even if they are due a refund! A taxpayer owing £10,000 in tax would pay £2,000 in fines, plus another £1,500 if they delayed paying until January 2020. So late filing can be a very expensive habit.

Tip: If facing a fine for late filing of a paper return, think about filing online to reduce the level of penalties. A 2017/18 paper return submitted on the 3rd of March 2019 would attract a £400 fine, but only £100 if filed online.

What Period?

There is a general concession that allows sole traders to draw up their accounts to March 31st instead of April 5th.

For most small businesses this is an advantage because not only is the 'end of March' an easier date to remember, you can effectively push five days' worth of income into the next tax year. And a deferral of tax is the next best thing to avoiding it altogether!

In some cases businesses that start up in the middle of the tax year prepare a complete 12 months of accounts from, say, 1 July 2017 to 30 June 2018. It is possible to prepare a tax return on this basis but, quite frankly it involves a lot more work.

It's far easier to have a short period from 1 July 2017 to 31 March 2018 and then use a financial year in sync with your tax year-end dates.

Whatever HMRC may say in their television ads, tax is 'taxing' so keep it simple where you can!

Which Form?

There are two different forms for self employment: the 'short' and the 'full'. The short form is only 2 pages long (SES in HMRC speak) and the full form (SEF) is 8 pages long. The two main criteria for using the short form are:

- Your total turnover for the year is under £85,000 (2017/18) or £7,083 per month if you have been trading for less than a year.

- You make your accounts up to the 5th April (or 31st March) each year.

There are also several other reasons for not being able to use the short form mentioned in the guidance notes ('SESN'), which apply to only a few taxpayers.

The biggest two groups of people unable to use the shorter version are probably those with a larger turnover, or those choosing to draw up accounts to dates other than the tax year end.

In Chapters 11, 12 and 13 I cover the short form in some detail and in Chapter 14 discuss the additional issues you need to consider with the full version.

The Future of Tax Returns – Making Tax Digital

The original idea for Making Tax Digital (MTD) was that all record keeping would need to be kept using commercial cloud accounting software. The current single annual tax return would be replaced with four quarterly updates, a final adjustment return, and then a further return for "other data".

Apparently this is supposed to be a time-saving "simplification".

Fortunately for the taxpayer, this project has been beset with delays and current indications are that it may not apply to businesses under the VAT for the foreseeable future. The chances of it applying to larger business anytime soon also seem increasingly slim, not least because there is currently no firm start date.

The official line at the time of writing was a start date "no earlier than April 2020". I would not be overly surprised to see the start date pushed back further and further. The only active element is for filing VAT returns which is covered in Section 6.

Accruals vs Cash Accounting

The bookkeeping records I have been showing you how to create are broadly constructed on the *accruals* basis.

The accruals basis is the standard way to prepare accounts. What matters under this system is the date you buy or sell an item. The date you pay your suppliers or receive payment is not relevant.

However, some unincorporated businesses (not companies or limited liability partnerships) can draw up their accounts using the 'cash basis'. This involves drawing up accounts based on the date transactions appear in the bank account, rather than the date on which purchases or sales take place.

Who is Eligible to Use the Cash Basis?

The cash basis is generally only available where the annual turnover (i.e. sales) of the business does not exceed £150,000. Those who are already using the cash basis may continue to do so provided their turnover does not exceed £300,000.

Advantages of Using the Cash Basis

The cash basis is generally easier to use because you don't need to worry about making too many accounting adjustments. You generally just add up everything that's gone in and out of your bank account during the year (and any other cash transactions, of course).

The cash basis is often the way people other than accountants see their finances, so many business owners will feel comfortable using it.

The cash basis has many advantages:

Simplicity

The key plus is that little accounting knowledge is required. To calculate your profit or loss for the tax year you simply tot up the transactions in your bank account and put them on your tax return. Then you can do something more interesting like de-scale the kettle.

Deferring Tax

If your customers take a long time to pay, your tax bill will be lower in the year you move to the cash basis.

Example

Anna receives average sales income of £2,000 per month but her customers are slow payers, taking on average 3 months to pay. Her declared income for 2016/17 under the accruals basis included all invoices raised from April 2016 to March 2017, totalling £24,000. However, by using the cash basis for 2017/18, she only has to include invoices paid in 2017/18. Anna doesn't need to "double count" those invoices already included in her 2016/17 return but paid during 2017/18.

Her computation would be as follows:

	£
Cash received 2017/18	24,000
Less included in 2016/17	6,000
Balance declared 2017/18	18,000

This gives Anna a one-off cash flow advantage. However, don't lose sight of the fact that she will eventually have to pay tax on the 'missing' £6,000 of income earned in 2017/18 but only received after the end of the tax year, so this is very much a tax deferral and not an absolute saving.

Bringing Forward Expenses & Delaying Income

Under the cash basis it is possible to 'game' your tax bill by bringing forward expenses or delaying the receipt of income until after the tax year has ended. This will allow you to defer paying tax by 12 months. For example, you could buy stock just before the end of the year.

Example

Leah runs a small shop and has net income of £43,000 a year. She buys stock twice a year in April and September, spending £10,000 in total per annum.

In 2017/18, under the cash basis, Leah brings forward both her April and September 2018 stock purchases and buys it all in March 2018.

Normal trading profits	*£ 43,000*
Less extra stock purchases	*£(10,000)*
Revised profits	*£ 33,000*

Despite stepping over boxes of stock for several months, Leah is rather pleased to be paying tax on lower profits for 2017/18, saving roughly £2,900 in income tax and National Insurance.

Drawbacks of Using the Cash Basis

Losses

If your business makes a loss, under the cash basis you can't offset that loss against your other income. This is potentially a significant issue for many types of start up business that might well show a loss under either accounting method in the first year, due to fixed overhead costs such as premises and equipment.

Volatile Profits

If you have "chunky" transactions, such as an annual stock purchase, rather than lots of small monthly transactions, you could end up with big swings in profits, like Leah in the above example. Not only could this leave you worse off in terms of income tax, there could also be an impact on the amount of child benefit you receive and your ability to obtain a loan or mortgage.

Example continued

Leah has still got some stock left at the end of March 2019. Due to a poor exchange rate she holds off buying any further stock until May 2019 (i.e. the 2019/20 tax year). Therefore, whilst the underlying performance of the business is unchanged, her expenses for 2018/19 are £10,000 lower than normal under the cash basis, resulting in a £53,000 profit, compared with the usual £43,000.

Leah's income now exceeds the UK higher-rate tax threshold (£46,350 for 2018/19) and she pays 42% income tax and National Insurance on £6,650 of income (she normally only pays 29%). She is understandably not very happy, even less so when she discovers that, as her taxable income exceeds £50,000, some of her child benefit is withdrawn as well.

Tax Deduction Limits

The cash basis has its benefits but one major drawback is that businesses are limited to a maximum claim of £500 per year for interest costs.

Where the cash basis is being used, there is generally no distinction between 'revenue expenditure' and 'capital expenditure' and capital expenditure can be claimed as it is paid.

However, from April 2017 new rules make it clear that no deduction will be allowed for:

- Non-depreciating assets (generally speaking, those expected to last more than 20 years)
- Assets that aren't for continuing use in the business
- Land (certain property fixtures are allowed)
- Financial assets
- Cars (motoring costs can be claimed in other ways)
- The cost of buying or selling a business
- Capital spending on education and training
- Intangible assets (e.g. intellectual property such as patents and trademarks) which last longer than 20 years

Sound Accounting

As many sole traders only prepare figures for the taxman, there is a risk of "dumbing down" your own record keeping if you use the cash basis and not recording as much data as would perhaps be helpful to understand how your business is performing.

Whilst for most people 'cash is king', it can disguise a slowly drowning business which is still generating positive cash flow but only by eating up its own capital, and equally depress the results of a profitable but growing business that is investing for the future.

Making the right decisions in such circumstances often depends on the owner understanding what is happening financially within the business, and the wrong data may result in the wrong commercial decisions.

So, in short, the 'simplification' of cash accounting creates more complexity by offering choices, but if you are a sole trader doing your own tax return with a straightforward business, it is probably a welcome simplification.

Preparing the Information

By following the bookkeeping guidelines in this book, there should be no mad panic to get your records up to date when the time comes to complete your tax return.

The main things you need to ensure are that:

- You have included all sales invoices for work undertaken during the tax year.

- You have included all purchase invoices for expenses you have incurred.

- Your bank account reconciles with the information in your accounting spreadsheet.

- You have worked out how much stock you have on hand, and what it cost you to buy if using accruals accounting.

Chapter 11

Case Study 1:
A Simple Service Business

To show you how to prepare your short self-employment tax return, let's bring back James and his book sales.

Last time we saw James, he had just started his business. Now he's reached the end of March and his sales and expenses sheets are laid out below. To keep it simple I've ignored all the intervening transactions (represented by cross hatching in the figures below). James will be preparing his accounts using the cash basis.

Sales

Figure 11.1 James's Sales: January 1st - March 31st 2018

Week	Description	Amount	Title One	Title Two	Title Three
01/01/2018	eBay	1,000.00	250.00	150.00	600.00
08/01/2018	eBay	250.00	150.00	50.00	50.00
08/01/2018	Website	100.00	25.00	25.00	50.00
25/03/2018	eBay	500.00	150.00	50.00	300.00
Total		3,650.00	950.00	600.00	2,100.00

Expenses

Figure 11.2 James's Expenses: January 1st - March 31st 2018

No.	Date	Payee	Description	Amount	Stationery	Paypal	eBay
1	05/01/2018	Staples	Office Supplies	59.50	59.50		
2	06/01/2018	PayPal	Transaction Fees	8.99		8.99	
3	08/01/2018	eBay	Seller's Fees	105.00			105.00
4	09/01/2018	PayPal	Transaction Fees	8.50		8.50	
28	31/03/2018	eBay	Seller's Fees	98.00			98.00
				-			
				541.20	81.50	66.70	393.00

I'm going to show you how to complete the self-employment pages of your 2017/18 tax return, using James's business as an example. This document consists of just two pages in which you have to provide details of your business income and expenses.

If you normally file a paper return as a sole trader, these pages will usually have been sent out to you automatically in April or May. If this is the first year you have been a sole trader you can download the forms from the HMRC website here:

www.gov.uk/government/publications/self-assessment-self-employment-short-sa103s

If you normally file your tax return online, the onscreen layout will be slightly different, and you won't receive any paper forms.

In the pages below we'll take a look at each of the tax return pages. It might be a good idea to go to the above web address and print out a copy now. Having it beside you while you read this chapter may make things a little easier.

Page SES1
Business Details

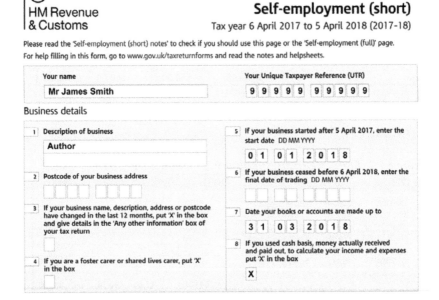

Illustrated above is the first half of page SES1, the first of the self-employment pages. Your name goes at the top left of this form and your 'Tax reference' at top right. The tax reference is a 10-digit code, also known as your 'Unique Taxpayer Reference' or UTR. This number should already be printed on the front left side of the first page of your tax return if you received one in the post. It usually also appears on any correspondence from HMRC.

If you have never registered as self-employed, you may not have a record set up and this will prevent you from filing online. When you submit your first return a UTR number will be allocated. You will find the following boxes under the "Business details" section of the self-employment page **SES1**:

- **Box 1** asks for a description of the business. You should try to be as specific as possible. The form doesn't ask you for the trading name of the business, but I would suggest you add this too if you have one and there is space to do so.

- **Box 2** is your business postcode. If you work from home you can leave this blank.

- **Box 3** asks you to put a note in the "Any other information" box of your tax return if any of the above details have changed. This is not relevant for James.

- **Box 4** asks a rather specific question about foster carers. If this applies to you please read the indicated guidance note.

- **Boxes 5 and 6** are for the start and end dates of trading. Box 5 is completed here with the date James started to trade – January 1st, when the first book contract was signed. Box 6 isn't relevant for James as he is still trading.

- **Box 7** shows the date the accounts are drawn up to. This is usually the same as the tax year. He started trading on January 1 2018 and, to keep things simple, chooses a tax year ending on March 31 2018.

- **Box 8** we need to tick as we are using the cash basis outlined in the previous chapter.

Business Income

Business income - if your annual business turnover was below £85,000

9 Your turnover - the takings, fees, sales or money earned by your business £ 3 6 5 0 · 0 0	**10.1** Trading income allowance - read the notes £ · 0 0
10 Any other business income not included in box 9 £ · 0 0	

There are only three boxes here. James simply transfers his total sales of £3,650 into box 9. There is no other income for box 10 but if there was sundry income excluded from his turnover he would enter it here. Box 10.1 we will look at after this example.

Allowable Business Expenses

Allowable business expenses
If your annual turnover was below £85,000 you may just put your total expenses in box 20, rather than filling in the whole section.

11 Costs of goods bought for resale or goods used £ · 0 0	**16** Accountancy, legal and other professional fees £ · 0 0
12 Car, van and travel expenses - after private use proportion £ · 0 0	**17** Interest and bank and credit card etc financial charges £ · 0 0
13 Wages, salaries and other staff costs £ · 0 0	**18** Phone, fax, stationery and other office costs £ · 0 0
14 Rent, rates, power and insurance costs £ · 0 0	**19** Other allowable business expenses - client entertaining costs aren't an allowable expense £ · 0 0
15 Repairs and maintenance of property and equipment £ · 0 0	**20** Total allowable expenses - total of boxes 11 to 19 £ 5 4 2 · 0 0

This section, still on page SES1, details business expenses.

If your turnover was under £85,000 you are able to simply put your total expenses in box 20 rather than having to provide a detailed breakdown in boxes 11 to 20.

What the form doesn't make clear is that this is an *annualised* figure. In other words, if you've only been trading for three months your annualised turnover will be greater than your actual turnover. In other words, your annualised turnover may be more than £85,000 even if your actual turnover isn't.

James has been trading for only three months. To work out whether he has to itemise his expenses, he takes the £85,000 limit and divides by 12 months. This gives him a figure of £7,083 per month. He then multiplies this by the three months he has been in business, giving him a figure of £21,250. This is considerably above his actual turnover of £3,650 and therefore James only has to provide his total expenses and doesn't have to split them into categories.

James therefore enters £542 in Box 20, being the total of his expenses for the period. You may notice that the shaded figure on the expenses spreadsheet (Figure 11.2) is £541.20 but the total in the tax return box is £542. This is due to the rather odd way HMRC handles rounding. Expenses are always rounded up and turnover is rounded down.

Page SES2

That's page one finished and onto page two which should be a little easier.

Net Profit or Loss

Net profit or loss

21	Net profit – *if your business income is more than your expenses (if box 9 + box 10 minus box 20 is positive)*	22	Or, net loss – *if your expenses exceed your business income (if box 20 minus (box 9 + box 10) is positive)*
£	3 1 0 8 · 0 0	£	· 0 0

There are two boxes in this section, 21 and 22. James has made a profit of £3,108, being the turnover of £3,650 in box 9 less the allowable expenses of £542 in box 20. This is entered as shown in box 21. Had James made a loss this would be entered in box 22.

Tax Allowances for Vehicles and Equipment (Capital Allowances)

Tax allowances for vehicles and equipment (capital allowances)
Don't include the cost of these in your business expenses.

23 Annual Investment Allowance	25 Other capital allowances
£ · 0 0	£ · 0 0
24 Allowance for small balance of unrelieved expenditure	26 Total balancing charges – for example, where you have disposed of items for more than their tax value
£ · 0 0	£ · 0 0

The next section on page SES2 deals with capital allowances. These allow you to claim a tax deduction for various assets such as computers and furniture, which depreciate in value over time.

This section is not relevant to James, so is left blank for now. However, we will return to this important section in a more detailed example in Chapter 14.

Calculating Your Taxable Profits

Calculating your taxable profits
Your taxable profit may not be the same as your net profit. Please read the 'Self-employment (short) notes' to see if you need to make any adjustments and fill in the boxes which apply to arrive at your taxable profit for the year.

27 Goods and/or services for your own use	29 Loss brought forward from earlier years set off against this year's profits – up to the amount in box 28
£ · 0 0	£ · 0 0
28 Net business profit for tax purposes (if box 21 + box 26 + box 27 minus (boxes 22 to 25) is positive). If you're claiming trading income allowance (box 21 + box 26 + box 27 minus box 10.1)	30 Any other business income not included in box 9 or box 10 – for example, non arm's length reverse premiums
£ 3 1 0 8 · 0 0	£ · 0 0

Total taxable profits or net business loss
If your total profits from all Self-employments and Partnerships for 2017-18 are less than £6,025, you don't have to pay Class 2 National Insurance contributions, but you may want to pay voluntarily (box 36) to protect your rights to certain benefits.

31 Total taxable profits from this business (if box 28 + box 30 minus box 29 is positive).	32 Net business loss for tax purposes (if boxes 22 to 25 minus (box 21 + box 26 + box 27) is positive)
£ 3 1 0 8 · 0 0	£ · 0 0

James simply brings his taxable profit of £3,108 from box 21 down to box 28 and down again to box 31.

No further entries in this section are required for James as his affairs are simple. I cover the other boxes in the next chapter, including how to deal with losses.

And that, believe it or not, is the extent of James's self-employment pages. The only thing left is to make sure you have ticked question two on page TR2 of the main return to show you have enclosed the self-employment pages and indicated how many sets of self employment pages are enclosed (one in this instance).

As a form-filling exercise it is quite straightforward once you know how to draw up your records and where the numbers go.

Form filling aside, what we haven't looked at is one major issue – are all the expenses tax deductible? And, just as important, are there any other expenses that are deductible that we haven't yet recorded in our records?

These sorts of questions are largely outside the scope of this book but are very important nonetheless. One thing we will cover is the new £1,000 trading income allowance available from April 2017.

Trading Income Allowance

The trading income allowance is available from the 2017/18 tax year.

This gives you an allowance for expenses of up to £1,000, regardless of your actual expenses.

So in this example, James can substitute his actual expenses of £542 for a sum of £1,000 in box 10.1. This reduces his profit from £3,108 to £2,650. Page SES1 will therefore looks as follows. You will note there is no entry for expenses in box 20.

Business income - if your annual business turnover was below £85,000

9	Your turnover - the takings, fees, sales or money earned by your business	10.1	Trading income allowance · read the notes
	£ 3 6 5 0 · 0 0		£ 1 0 0 0 · 0 0

10	Any other business income not included in box 9
	£ · 0 0

Allowable business expenses

If your annual turnover was below £85,000 you may just put your total expenses in box 20, rather than filling in the whole section.

11	Costs of goods bought for resale or goods used	16	Accountancy, legal and other professional fees
	£ · 0 0		£ · 0 0

12	Car, van and travel expenses – after private use proportion	17	Interest and bank and credit card etc financial charges
	£ · 0 0		£ · 0 0

13	Wages, salaries and other staff costs	18	Phone, fax, stationery and other office costs
	£ · 0 0		£ · 0 0

14	Rent, rates, power and insurance costs	19	Other allowable business expenses – client entertaining costs aren't an allowable expense
	£ · 0 0		£ · 0 0

15	Repairs and maintenance of property and equipment	20	Total allowable expenses - total of boxes 11 to 19
	£ · 0 0		£ · 0 0

The reduction in net income of £458 will also reduce James's tax bill, so he is quite happy to have spotted this allowance!

A few further points about the allowance:

- A claim needs to be made, it is not automatic. However, it would normally be to your benefit to make the claim if your expenses are below £1,000.
- The full allowance is available even if your business was only trading for part of the year.
- You can't use the allowance to generate a loss, so in practice if your turnover is under £1,000, you claim up to the value of your turnover.
- If you have two or more sole trades only one allowance of £1,000 is available. The good news is the allowance can be allocated between each trade. The bad news is you can't claim normal expenses for one sole trade and the trading income allowance for another: you must make the same choice for both trades.
- If as a result of the allowance your profit is nil (that is to say your turnover is £1,000 or less), you may not meet the criteria for self-assessment.

Chapter 12

Case Study 2:
A Simple Stock Business

Having warmed up with an easy example it's time to tackle something a little more involved. Step forward Emily and her art business. Business for Emily has been growing fast. Figures 12.1 and 12.2 show her sales and stock spreadsheets:

Figure 12.1 Emily's Sales Spreadsheet

Ref	Invoice Date	Customer	Artist	Amount	Paid Date	Cost	Gross Profit
INV001	01/01/2018	Mr A	Anna	1,000.00	08/01/2018	700.00	300.00
INV002	02/01/2018	Mr C	Paul	250.00	22/01/2018	100.00	150.00
INV003	05/01/2018	Mrs D	Peter	100.00	Bad	25.00	75.00
INV017	20/03/2018	Mr Y	Ali	500.00	25/03/2018	300.00	200.00
INV018	25/03/2018	Mrs Z	Kai	700.00	o/s	450.00	250.00
Total				12,150.00		9,500.00	2,650.00

Figure 12.2 Emily's Stock Spreadsheet

Date Purchased	Artist	Item Name	Purchase Price	Date Sold	Stock Value
01/12/2017	Anna	Flowers	700.00	01/01/2018	-
01/12/2017	Paul	Seascape	100.00	02/01/2018	-
01/12/2017	Peter	Calm	25.00	05/01/2018	-
01/12/2017	John	Face	400.00	22/02/2018	-
25/03/2018	Anna	Vase	500.00	Stock	500.00
	Total		10,000.00		500.00

An abridged version of her expenses spreadsheet is shown in Figure 12.3. (I have shaded out the descriptions and a number of the transactions so we just have a few lines as an example.)

Figure 12.3 Emily's Expenses Spreadsheet

No.	Total	Stock	Drawings	Shipping	Admin	Interest	Advert	Travel	Rent
1	300	300							
2	200						200		
3	50							50	
4	100								100
52	500.00	500.00							
	-								
	17,978.00	10,000.00	5,000.00	100.00	75.00	- 12.00	575.00	240.00	2,000.00

Immediately we can see there is quite a bit more information to deal with, which means her tax return is going to be a little more complicated.

Page SES1
Business Details

HM Revenue & Customs

Self-employment (short)

Tax year 6 April 2017 to 5 April 2018 (2017-18)

Please read the 'Self-employment (short) notes' to check if you should use this page or the 'Self-employment (full)' page.
For help filling in this form, go to www.gov.uk/taxreturnforms and read the notes and helpsheets.

Your name

Miss Emily Chapman

Your Unique Taxpayer Reference (UTR)

6 6 6 6 6 6 6 6 6 6

Business details

1 Description of business

Art Retailer

2 Postcode of your business address

PO1   2LA

3 If your business name, description, address or postcode have changed in the last 12 months, put 'X' in the box and give details in the 'Any other information' box of your tax return

4 If you are a foster carer or shared lives carer, put 'X' in the box

5 If your business started after 5 April 2017, enter the start date DD MM YYYY

0 1 0 1 2 0 1 8

6 If your business ceased before 6 April 2018, enter the final date of trading DD MM YYYY

7 Date your books or accounts are made up to

3 1 0 3 2 0 1 8

8 If you used cash basis, money actually received and paid out, to calculate your income and expenses put 'X' in the box

The first page of the self-employment pages is much the same as in the previous example, with Emily's business covering the same time period as James.

The post code for her business address is entered into box 2. The rest of the address isn't actually required.

Since her turnover is below £85,000 on an annualised basis (it is £12,150 over three months or £48,600 per annum), she is also eligible for the 'short' rather than the 'full' return.

Because Emily's turnover is below £150,000 she can elect to use the cash basis. However, this example uses the *accruals* basis, which for a stock business is probably the most sensible. Emily has therefore not ticked box 8.

Business Income

Business income - if your annual business turnover was below £85,000

9 Your turnover - the takings, fees, sales or money earned by your business	10.1 Trading income allowance - read the notes
£ 1 2 1 5 0 · 0 0	£ · 0 0
10 Any other business income not included in box 9	
£ 1 2 · 0 0	

Again this is fairly straightforward. Emily simply transfers her total sales of £12,150 into box 9.

Box 10 also applies this time. If you look at the expenses spreadsheet (Figure 12.3), there is a negative number '-12.00' in the 'Interest' column. Instead of having interest as an expense (for example on a business loan) Emily has earned interest and therefore has some extra income to report. She has included this in the box 10 figure.

The interest could equally as well be shown on box 1 on page TR3 of the main return. If you have significant amounts of interest (more than about £50 say), I suggest you show it on page TR3 rather than here, as you will benefit from any tax deducted by the bank which isn't taken into account if entered in box 10.

A claim under Box 10.1 is not helpful, as Emily's expenses are more than £1,000. There is more about the trading income allowance in the previous chapter.

Allowable Business Expenses

11 Costs of goods bought for resale or goods used		**16** Accountancy, legal and other professional fees
£ 9 6 0 0 . 0 0		£ . 0 0
12 Car, van and travel expenses – after private use proportion		**17** Interest and bank and credit card etc financial charges
£ 2 1 5 . 0 0		£ . 0 0
13 Wages, salaries and other staff costs		**18** Phone, fax, stationery and other office costs
£ . 0 0		£ 7 5 . 0 0
14 Rent, rates, power and insurance costs		**19** Other allowable business expenses – client entertaining costs aren't an allowable expense
£ 2 0 0 0 . 0 0		£ 6 7 5 . 0 0
15 Repairs and maintenance of property and equipment		**20** Total allowable expenses – total of boxes 11 to 19
£ . 0 0		£ 1 2 5 6 5 . 0 0

As Emily's turnover is less than £85,000 on an annualised basis (it would be £48,600 as computed above if prorated over the whole year), she does not have to fill in boxes 11 to 19. She could just put her total expenses in box 20, as we did for James previously. I have, however, chosen to report each of the figures in this example to show you how it is done and also to help those of you who might need to fill in the full form.

If you want to know exactly what expenses go in each of the different categories, for example if you want to know what expenses to enter in box 14 for Rent, rates, power and insurance costs, you'll find more detailed information in Appendix 2.

Box 11 Cost of goods bought for resale or goods used

Let's kick off with the cost of sales, which are entered in **box 11**. For a retailer like Emily this is simply the purchase cost of all the stock she has sold during the year. If she was a manufacturer, for example if she painted the pictures herself, her cost of sales would be the cost of the raw materials: paint, canvas, picture frames, paint brushes etc.

The purchase cost of the paintings she has sold can be found on the sales spreadsheet (Figure 12.1), which lists how much Emily has paid for each of the paintings she sold. The total is £9,500.

We can also check the accuracy of this figure by looking at the stock spreadsheet, which shows the value of stock on hand at the end of the financial year and the total value of stock purchased:

	£
Total value of purchases	*10,000*
Less: value of stock at year-end	*(500)*
Cost of Goods Sold	*9,500*

This method shows the value of keeping slightly more records than you actually require, as you can double check the accuracy of your figures. In practice there could be other adjustments for things like damaged stock.

Thinking more widely about direct expenses, these are costs that vary directly in line with sales. It would not include rent, for example, because she would pay that even if she didn't sell any paintings.

It would include, for example, shipping costs or any commissions paid to other people who help her sell the paintings – in other words, costs that are directly related to selling the paintings. In Emily's case the amount spent on shipping is £100. The cost of shipping goods both to the end customer and for stock arriving at your shop is a "cost of sale" and included in this box.

Emily therefore enters into box 11 £9,600, comprising £9,500 for the stock sold, plus £100 for sending it out to customers.

Box 12 Car, van and travel expenses

This box includes travel and subsistence and business travel. In Emily's case the £240 includes bed and breakfast expenses, a train fare incurred meeting a supplier plus a £25 parking fine.

This parking fine is unfortunately not allowable for tax purposes. The £25 disallowable item is deducted before the entry of £215 you can see in box 12.

	£
Total travel expenses per Fig 12.3	*240*
Less Disallowable parking fine	*(25)*
Allowable amount in box 12	*215*

If Emily used her car for business purposes the amounts would be entered here. For businesses under the VAT threshold there is the option of either:

- Claiming a share of the actual costs of the vehicle in proportion to the business and private usage, or

- Claiming mileage at a rate of 45p per business mile for the first 10,000 miles and 25p thereafter.

Which method is more beneficial to you will depend on your circumstances. Claiming a share of actual costs is quite complicated and I recommend reading the guidance notes that come with your self assessment return if you plan to tackle this yourself. A proportion of the actual cost of the vehicle will be entered into box 25 "other capital allowances" with the running costs entered in box 12.

Box 13 Wages, salaries and other staff costs

Emily doesn't have any employees, so **box 13** is left blank. If she did have employees she would put all the wages, employee benefits, national insurance contributions, recruitment agency fees and other staff-related costs in this box. This box won't contain her own national insurance contributions as these are not tax deductible.

You should note that 'drawings' (money taken out of the business by Emily for her personal use) are not included as an employee expense. Sole traders are not employees of their own businesses and cannot pay themselves a salary.

Instead they take drawings that are withdrawals of profit from the business. Because profits are calculated after deducting all expenses, the drawings themselves are not a business expense.

Box 14 Rent, rates, power and insurance costs

Emily has paid £2,000 in rent and this goes into **box 14**. In practice she would also have other premises costs such as business rates, electricity and gas, and insurance premiums. These would all go in box 14.

Box 15 Repairs and renewals of property and equipment

This would include repairs she has to make to her business premises or any equipment she uses in the business. Again in this example this box is left blank for Emily.

Box 16 Accountancy, legal and other professional fees

Legal and professional costs would be used for fees such as using a solicitor to draw up terms and conditions or accountancy fees for helping with your returns.

Box 17 Interest and bank and credit card etc. financial charges

This is for interest paid, such as on an overdraft or bank loan and other finance charges. You would also include related fees such as bank charges and overdraft fees you may incur. Fortunately Emily doesn't have any of these costs.

Box 18 Phone, fax, stationery and other office costs

This is for general administrative expenses such as stationery and other office expenses. Emily has £75 to include here.

Box 19 Other allowable business expenses

This is the 'catch all' box for anything not entered into boxes 11 to 18. For Emily this includes £575 for advertising she has incurred promoting her business, mainly some flyers and some printed adverts in magazines.

There is also £100 for bad debts. This represents the unpaid invoice INV003 to Mrs D shown in Figure 12.1. We know Mrs D is in serious financial difficulties (she has been declared bankrupt) and there is very little chance of this debt being paid.

We can therefore safely 'write off' the debt. This is different to the outstanding INV018 for Mrs Z, which we expect to be paid in a few days.

Box 20 Total allowable expenses

This is simply the total of boxes 11 to 19. We will see below in 'final checks' how to ensure that this is actually the correct figure!

Using Your Spreadsheets

All of the above expense information was extracted with relative ease from the expenses spreadsheet in Figure 12.3.

In practice, what often happens is that you will have many more expense categories in your spreadsheet than there are on the tax return. This means several categories will have to be added together.

For example, you may list your phone bills and stationery separately, but they would both go under the "Phone, fax, stationery and other office costs" heading.

The trick is to always have too many and not too few categories. There is nothing worse than having to split, say, your motor expenses from your other travel and subsistence retrospectively.

In practice, it's worth making a note in your bookkeeping records to show in which tax return box number each expense category has been included. This will provide an 'audit trail' if HMRC ever enquires into your return and you need to work out what you did 2 or 3 years previously.

SES2

Onto the second page of the return.

Net Profit or Loss

Net profit or loss

21 Net profit – if your business income is more than your expenses (if box 9 + box 10 minus box 20 is positive)	22 Or, net loss – if your expenses exceed your business income (if box 20 minus (box 9 + box 10) is positive)
£ · 0 0	£ 4 0 3 · 0 0

To calculate the net profit or loss we take the total incomes (boxes 9 and 10) and deduct the total expenses (box 20) as follows:

Sales Income + Other Income – Total Expenses = Net Profit or Loss

Boxes 9 + 10 – 20 = Box 21 or Box 22

£12,150 + £12 – £12,565 = – £403

Had Emily made a profit, this would be entered into box 21 as in the example of James above. As it is a loss it goes into box 22.

Tax Allowances for Vehicles and Equipment (Capital Allowances)

This section is not relevant to Emily but is covered in Chapter 14.

Calculating Your Taxable Profits

Calculating your taxable profits

Your taxable profit may not be the same as your net profit. Please read the 'Self-employment (short) notes' to see if you need to make any adjustments and fill in the boxes which apply to arrive at your taxable profit for the year.

27 Goods and/or services for your own use	29 Loss brought forward from earlier years set off against this year's profits – up to the amount in box 28
£ 2 0 0 · 0 0	£ · 0 0
28 Net business profit for tax purposes (if box 21 + box 26 + box 27 minus (boxes 22 to 25) is positive). If you're claiming trading income allowance (box 21 + box 26 + box 27 minus box 10.1)	30 Any other business income not included in box 9 or box 10 – for example, non arm's length reverse premiums
£ · 0 0	£ · 0 0

Total taxable profits or net business loss

If your total profits from all Self-employments and Partnerships for 2017-18 are less than £6,025, you don't have to pay Class 2 National Insurance contributions, but you may want to pay voluntarily (box 36) to protect your rights to certain benefits.

31 Total taxable profits from this business (if box 28 + box 30 minus box 29 is positive).	32 Net business loss for tax purposes (if boxes 22 to 25 minus (box 21 + box 26 + box 27) is positive)
£ · 0 0	£ 2 0 3 · 0 0

This section works out any further adjustments to taxable income.

Box 27 is used where a sole trader takes goods for their own use. Emily has taken goods with a resale value of £200 and used them at home, and therefore has entered £200 in box 27. You should note that following a court case in recent years it is now the *sales price* and not the purchase price that is supposed to be used when adjusting for goods or services for your own use. Historically the purchase price of the goods was used.

Box 28 would show the taxable profit if Emily had made one. However, in this example even after the adjustment for goods for personal use Emily has still got a tax loss of £203.

Box 29 is where losses bought forward from earlier years are entered. As Emily is in her first year there is no entry here but as her losses will be carried forward to the following year, she will have an entry in this box next time around.

Box 30 is another 'catch all' box aimed at picking up any other income not already entered.

Box 31 would again show the taxable profit taken from box 28, as adjusted for any entries in boxes 29 and 30.

Box 32 is used when there is a taxable loss. In Emily's case this is £203.

box 22 + box 27 = box 32

£-403 + £200 = -£203

Losses, Class 4 NICs and Deductions

Losses, Class 2 and Class 4 National Insurance contributions (NICs) and CIS deductions
If you've made a loss for tax purposes (box 32), read the 'Self-employment (short) notes' and fill in boxes 33 to 35 as appropriate.

33 Loss from this tax year set off against other income for 2017-18 £ . 0 0		**36** If your total profits for 2017-18 are less than £6,025 and you choose to pay Class 2 NICs voluntarily, put 'X' in the box
34 Loss to be carried back to previous year(s) and set off against income (or capital gains) £ . 0 0		**37** If you're exempt from paying Class 4 NICs, put 'X' in the box
35 Total loss to carry forward after all other set-offs – including unused losses brought forward £ 2 0 3 . 0 0		**38** Total Construction Industry Scheme (CIS) deductions taken from your payments by contractors – CIS subcontractors only £ . 0 0

Boxes 33 to 35 are concerned with the use of any losses as a sole trader.

The basic theory is that you can offset trading losses against certain other income in the current year, for example a salary if you have one (**box 33**). This may get you immediate tax relief, in other words, real money back from the taxman!

You can carry a loss back to the previous tax year if you had a profit then (**box 34**), or if you have no profits in the prior year and nothing to offset it against in the current year, you can carry the loss forward to a future period (**box 35**).

The tax treatment of losses can get quite complicated. If you have one you should think about getting some help from an accountant to ensure you make the most of it. In Emily's case, she has chosen to carry her losses forward to the next tax year (box 35) because she doesn't have any other PAYE income in the current period to offset the loss against and obtain a tax refund.

In the following year's tax return this £203 will appear in box 29.

Box 36 is *optional* for Emily as she made a loss and she has left it blank. If she had ticked it, the Class 2 National Insurance for the whole of the 2017/18 tax year would have been £148.20.

Why volunteer to pay more National Insurance than required I hear you ask? "Pensions" is the answer. Under the current system you need 35 "qualifying years" for a full state pension – broadly speaking years in which you have paid National Insurance. If you're not sure how many qualifying years you have and are worried about not having enough, go here for further details:

www.gov.uk/new-state-pension

Class 2 National Insurance was meant to be scrapped this year (2018/19) but its abolition has been postponed until 2019/20.

Box 37 may be ticked if you are exempt. This applies broadly to young entrepreneurs under 16 and those at the other end of the scale who have reached state pension age.

Box 38 is relevant to subcontractors in the construction industry scheme (CIS scheme) who have tax deducted from their wages before they are paid. The value of the tax deducted goes in this box.

Further initial guidance is available within the general help sheet "Self-employment (short) notes" which is posted to you with the paper copy of your tax return or is available to download from the HMRC website:

gov.uk/government/publications/self-assessment-self-employment-short-sa103s

Final Checks

Once you have got all the numbers on to your tax return it makes a lot of sense to refer back to the source documents and check that everything stacks up and you haven't left anything out.

We originally had:

	£
Sales	12,150
Less total expenses	(17,978)
Unadjusted loss	(5,828)
Add back stock	500
Add back drawings	5,000
Add back parking fine	25
Add back stock for own use	200
Less bad debts	(100)
Net loss	(203)

The net loss calculated this way is, thankfully, the same as that appearing on the tax return in box 32.

If you are doing your own tax return, it is well worth persevering with this sort of check to ensure you have got all the numbers into your return and added everything up correctly.

I know this example has got a lot more complicated than the example with James, but it does demonstrate that things get a lot trickier once you throw in a few real-life issues and some adjustments are required.

It is perhaps worth coming back to the point that it was not compulsory for Emily to fill in the expenses by individual category in boxes 11 to 19. She could have just entered the total in box 20 as her turnover was below £85,000.

Many people ask me whether it's a good idea to fill in all this extra detail or not. It is entirely up to you but I find the extra bit of effort can pay off as it may help you spot an omitted expense. It is a lot easier to spot an omission in the form of an empty line on your tax return as opposed to one that is buried in a total figure. Little things like this can help you reduce your tax bill.

Chapter 13

Case Study 3: A Simple Stock Business - Cash Basis

Having shown you the accruals basis for Emily in some detail, in this chapter I will look at the same data under the alternative cash basis. The cash basis is in many ways a more logical approach for taxpayers who don't use an accountant to complete their tax returns as you can simply "follow the cash".

I summarise below the key differences between cash and accruals:

	Cash Basis	**Accruals Basis**
Income	Date of payment	Date the work is carried out or date item sold
Expense (stock item)	Date of payment	Date stock sold (matching to sale)
Expense (overhead)	Date of payment	Match to the period, eg rent would match the rental period covered by the payment

Let us look again at Emily's sales spreadsheet. This was initially created with accruals accounting in mind:

Figure 13.1 Emily's Original Sales Spreadsheet

Ref	Invoice Date	Customer	Artist	Amount	Paid Date	Cost	Gross Profit
INV001	01/01/2018	Mr A	Anna	1,000.00	08/01/2018	700.00	300.00
INV002	02/01/2018	Mr C	Paul	250.00	22/01/2018	100.00	150.00
INV003	05/01/2018	Mrs D	Peter	100.00	Bad	25.00	75.00
INV017	20/03/2018	Mr Y	Ali	500.00	25/03/2018	300.00	200.00
INV018	25/03/2018	Mrs Z	Kai	700.00	o/s	450.00	250.00
Total				12,150.00		9,500.00	2,650.00

We can see the "Amount" column lists the items sold during the period, but not all the invoices have been paid.

To work out Emily's sales under the cash basis we 'add back' her unpaid invoices as follows:

	£
Sales records	12,150
Outstanding invoices	(700)
Bad debts	(100)
Net payments received	11,350

"Hang on a minute" you are probably saying, isn't the cash basis supposed to be easier?

"Yes" is the answer, but only if you start from the right point.

What Emily actually needs to do is go back to basics with her record keeping. In the earlier chapters we considered the information needs for your record keeping. As there are different information needs for each method, it follows logically that you will need to keep slightly different records.

Under cash accounting Emily needs to capture the data to show when she gets paid, not when she sends out an invoice. This can be done in several ways including:

- Adding a "Paid period" column to the spreadsheet to record in which tax year payments are received. This is probably most relevant for a business which receives a mixture of bank payments and cash payments.

- Recording data directly from the bank account. This would be good for a business that receives most of its payments via the bank and doesn't need to record invoices issued.

  Remember, of course, if you are working from the bank account you would also need to add in any cash payments received and deduct payments into your bank account that are not sales income. For example, if you received a business loan or had to put some of your own money into the business to see it through a tough patch, these amounts would not be included as part of your business turnover.

Emily would like to track her sales invoices and decides to amend her spreadsheet by adding a new column "Paid 2017/18".

Figure 13.2 Emily's Revised Sales Spreadsheet

Ref	Invoice Date	Customer	Artist	Amount	Paid Date	Paid 2017/18	Outstanding
INV001	01/01/2018	Mr A	Anna	1,000.00	08/01/2018	1,000.00	
INV002	02/01/2018	Mr C	Paul	250.00	22/01/2018	250.00	
INV003	05/01/2018	Mrs D	Peter	100.00	Bad		100.00
INV017	20/03/2018	Mr Y	Ali	500.00	25/03/2018	500.00	
INV018	25/03/2018	Mrs Z	Kai	700.00	o/s		700.00
Total				12,150.00		11,350.00	800.00

Emily checks the £11,350 from the "Paid 2017/18" column matches the cash paid into her bank account and we have our first number to enter on the tax return. I have entered the other data as in the previous example and ticked box 8 for cash accounting.

HM Revenue & Customs

Self-employment (short)

Tax year 6 April 2017 to 5 April 2018 (2017-18)

Please read the 'Self-employment (short) notes' to check if you should use this page or the 'Self-employment (full)' page. For help filling in this form, go to www.gov.uk/taxreturnforms and read the notes and helpsheets.

Your name	Your Unique Taxpayer Reference (UTR)
Miss Emily Chapman	6 6 6 6 6 6 6 6

Business details

1 Description of business

Art Retailer

2 Postcode of your business address

P O 1   2 L A

3 If your business name, description, address or postcode have changed in the last 12 months, put 'X' in the box and give details in the 'Any other information' box of your tax return

4 If you are a foster carer or shared lives carer, put 'X' in the box

5 If your business started after 5 April 2017, enter the start date DD MM YYYY

0 1 0 1 2 0 1 8

6 If your business ceased before 6 April 2018, enter the final date of trading DD MM YYYY

7 Date your books or accounts are made up to

3 1 0 3 2 0 1 8

8 If you used cash basis, money actually received and paid out, to calculate your income and expenses put 'X' in the box

X

Business income – if your annual business turnover was below £85,000

9 Your turnover – the takings, fees, sales or money earned by your business

£ 1 1 3 5 0 · 0 0

10.1 Trading income allowance - read the notes

£   · 0 0

10 Any other business income not included in box 9

£   1 2 · 0 0

Allowable Business Expenses

This is Emily's expenses spreadsheet as previously:

Figure 13.3 Emily's Expenses Spreadsheet

No.	Total	Stock	Drawings	Shipping	Admin	Interest	Advert	Travel	Rent
1	300	300							
2	200						200		
3	50							50	
4	100								100
52	500.00	500.00							
	-								
	17,978.00	10,000.00	5,000.00	100.00	75.00	- 12.00	575.00	240.00	2,000.00

This translates as follows onto the actual tax return:

Allowable business expenses

If your annual turnover was below £85,000 you may just put your total expenses in box 20, rather than filling in the whole section.

11 Costs of goods bought for resale or goods used	16 Accountancy, legal and other professional fees
£ 1 0 1 0 0 · 0 0	£ · 0 0
12 Car, van and travel expenses – after private use proportion	17 Interest and bank and credit card etc financial charges
£ 2 1 5 · 0 0	£ · 0 0
13 Wages, salaries and other staff costs	18 Phone, fax, stationery and other office costs
£ · 0 0	£ 7 5 · 0 0
14 Rent, rates, power and insurance costs	19 Other allowable business expenses – client entertaining costs aren't an allowable expense
£ 2 0 0 0 · 0 0	£ 5 7 5 · 0 0
15 Repairs and maintenance of property and equipment	20 Total allowable expenses – total of boxes 11 to 19
£ · 0 0	£ 1 2 9 6 5 · 0 0

The majority of the data is the same as in the previous chapter. However, **Box 11** *Cost of goods bought for resale or goods used* now shows £10,100.

This is because we are merely concerned with the overall stock purchase – which we know from the expenses sheet in Figure 13.3 is £10,000 plus the £100 shipping cost.

No adjustments are required for stock on hand at the end of the period.

Box 19 *Other allowable business expenses* shows just the advertising costs of £575. The earlier accruals example showed £675, including the bad debt of £100.

Under cash accounting bad debts require no entry as no transaction appears in the bank account. There is just an initial "promise to pay".

You may recall that, under accruals accounting, the £100 sale or "promise to pay" was recorded in box 9 (turnover) and the bad debt in box 19 (other allowable expenses), with the two amounts cancelling each other out. The result is the same – no profit or loss – but the amounts are recorded in a different way.

The remainder of the entries remain unchanged.

SES2

Onto the second page of the return, and it is much as before, with the exception of deciding to pay voluntary Class 2 National Insurance by ticking box 36.

Net profit or loss

21 Net profit - if your business income is more than your expenses (if box 9 + box 10 minus box 20 is positive)	22 Or, net loss - if your expenses exceed your business income (if box 20 minus (box 9 + box 10) is positive)
£ ⸱ 0 0	£ 1 6 0 3 ⸱ 0 0

Tax allowances for vehicles and equipment (capital allowances)
Don't include the cost of these in your business expenses.

23 Annual Investment Allowance	25 Other capital allowances
£ ⸱ 0 0	£ ⸱ 0 0
24 Allowance for small balance of unrelieved expenditure	26 Total balancing charges - for example, where you have disposed of items for more than their tax value
£ ⸱ 0 0	£ ⸱ 0 0

Calculating your taxable profits
Your taxable profit may not be the same as your net profit. Please read the 'Self-employment (short) notes' to see if you need to make any adjustments and fill in the boxes which apply to arrive at your taxable profit for the year.

27 Goods and/or services for your own use	29 Loss brought forward from earlier years set off against this year's profits - up to the amount in box 28
£ 2 0 0 ⸱ 0 0	£ ⸱ 0 0
28 Net business profit for tax purposes (if box 21 + box 26 + box 27 minus (boxes 22 to 25) is positive). If you're claiming trading income allowance (box 21 + box 26 + box 27 minus box 10.1)	30 Any other business income not included in box 9 or box 10 - for example, non arm's length reverse premiums
£ ⸱ 0 0	£ ⸱ 0 0

Total taxable profits or net business loss
If your total profits from all Self-employments and Partnerships for 2017-18 are less than £6,025, you don't have to pay Class 2 National Insurance contributions, but you may want to pay voluntarily (box 36) to protect your rights to certain benefits.

31 Total taxable profits from this business (if box 28 + box 30 minus box 29 is positive).	32 Net business loss for tax purposes (if boxes 22 to 25 minus (box 21 + box 26 + box 27) is positive)
£ ⸱ 0 0	£ 1 4 0 3 ⸱ 0 0

Losses, Class 2 and Class 4 National Insurance contributions (NICs) and CIS deductions

If you've made a loss for tax purposes (box 32), read the 'Self-employment (short) notes' and fill in boxes 33 to 35 as appropriate.

33 Loss from this tax year set off against other income for 2017–18 £ [ ][ ][ ][ ][ ][ ] · 0 0		**36** If your total profits for 2017–18 are less than £6,025 and you choose to pay Class 2 NICs voluntarily, put 'X' in the box **X**	
34 Loss to be carried back to previous year(s) and set off against income (or capital gains) £ [ ][ ][ ][ ][ ][ ] · 0 0		**37** If you're exempt from paying Class 4 NICs, put 'X' in the box [ ]	
35 Total loss to carry forward after all other set-offs – including unused losses brought forward £ [ ] 1 4 0 3 · 0 0		**38** Total Construction Industry Scheme (CIS) deductions taken from your payments by contractors – CIS subcontractors only £ [ ][ ][ ][ ][ ][ ] · 0 0	

Under the cash basis, the loss of £1,403 cannot be offset against your other income (box 33) as is possible under the accruals basis. In other words, unlike the accruals basis, you can't use the loss to reduce your tax bill on other sources of income such as salary income. This may be an important consideration when deciding which method to use.

Final Checks

Now Emily has got what she hopes are the correct numbers on her tax return it makes a lot of sense to refer back to the original bookkeeping records and check we haven't done anything silly:

We originally had:

	£
Sales	*11,350*
Less total expenses	*(17,978)*
Unadjusted loss	*(6,628)*
Add back drawings	*5,000*
Add back parking fine	*25*
Add back stock for own use	*200*
Net loss	*(1,403)*

The net loss calculated this way is the same as that appearing on the tax return in box 32.

Emily can use her business bank account to tot up her annual deposits and withdrawals and check whether it all comes out right. Even if she cannot reconcile everything "to the penny", she should be able to get pretty close to the total sales figures and total expenses figures and therefore have some comfort that the figures on her tax return are about right.

In terms of "sanity checking" the return, it also helps that Emily has filled in the expenses by individual category in boxes 11 to 19. She could have just entered the total in box 20 and not bothered with more detail, but this would have been dangerous if she just entered the £17,978 without properly considering what made up that total. A little bit of detail goes a long way.

Summary

Having gone through this example we have some emerging principles with respect to the differences between the cash basis and the accruals basis:

- There are fewer adjustments under the cash basis

- You need to set up your records to deliver the correct data for your chosen method

- Under the cash basis expenses - which most small business tend to pay quickly - go in when paid

- Under the cash basis sales - which can often take a while to be paid – are only counted when you have received the money

The net effect of "cash vs accruals" will vary from business to business but the tendency will be for the cash basis to increase losses in the earlier years during the set up and early growth phases.

You may therefore save some tax in the crucial early years of the business which might aid your cash flow. However, if the cash basis reduces your reported profits, it will inevitably make it harder to get loans or other forms of finance too, so there are downsides.

You should therefore consider what result you wish to achieve, which ought to be the starting point for anyone preparing a set of accounts.

Finally, if you are completing your own tax return the key things to remember are:

- Declare all income (either this year or next, where allowed)
- Don't double count expenses
- Be consistent - account for things the same way each year
- Get your return in on time
- Do something more fun when you are finished!

Chapter 14

Further Self-Assessment Issues

This chapter covers some more advanced topics you may need to understand to complete your own tax return.

Accruals and Prepayments

It's important to understand the basic accounting conventions of matching income and expenditure to the period in which they relate.

Typically, if you undertake long-term projects you may be in the middle of several jobs at the end of the year. In this instance you are obliged (under accruals accounting conventions) to estimate how much of the project has been completed, and therefore how much money you have earned but not billed.

Example

Richard designs websites. He has already sent out invoices totalling £20,000 and has three projects ongoing:

- *He is half way through a £5,000 web development project for Andrew, having billed £1,000.*

- *He has billed £500 towards a £2,000 site for Mary but has barely started the project.*

- *He has billed Paul for £2,000. Only £1,800 has been paid as there is a three-month retention period.*

For Andrew's project he has effectively earned £2,500 (i.e. half) and billed £1,000 and therefore needs to add £1,500 to his sales.

For Mary's project he has billed in advance and needs to deduct £500 as he hasn't actually done anything yet.

For Paul's project the site is complete and the £2,000 invoice has been sent out. Only if the site wasn't properly finished would there be any adjustment here. So the total income is:

	£
Sales per spreadsheet	20,000
Accrual for Andrew	1,500
Less prepayment Mary	(500)
Total income	21,000

In the following year Andrew must remember to take off the £1,500 current year accrual from his income or he will be double counting his income.

This is often when people get confused when doing their own accounts. So if you need to make this sort of adjustment it may be worth getting help.

A similar principle applies to your expenses. For example, Emily in Chapter 12 paid out £2,000 in rent. If this was paid out on March 1, for the three months March to May, only one-third (£667) would be tax deductible in the tax year to the end of March. The remaining £1,333 would have to be claimed in the following year.

Capital Allowances

To keep matters as simple as possible in the previous examples, I skirted around the capital allowances section on page SES2. In practice, most businesses are entitled to claim these allowances.

In accounting terms, there is a distinction between 'revenue expenses' and 'capital expenses'. In short, a revenue expense is spending on something that is 'used up' quickly, for example stationery or a train ticket.

A capital expense is something that will last longer than a year, for example a car, computer or building. Furthermore, capital items are normally substantial items rather than low-value items. For example, you wouldn't treat the purchase of a wastebasket as a capital expense, even if you get 20 years' life out of it.

The accounting reason why we have capital items is so that the cost of certain 'capital' items can be spread over a number of years and matched with the income they help create, rather than subtracting the whole cost in year one. This then gives you a better understanding of the costs of the business.

However, the accounting treatment does not always follow the tax treatment, which is now balanced so that most capital assets will actually get a full tax deduction in the first year.

All businesses are entitled to an "annual investment allowance" of up to £200,000. This means in practice that any spending on capital goods by a small business (with some exceptions including cars and buildings) will be fully tax deductible in the year incurred, even if for accounting purposes it is treated as a capital asset.

The only "funny" is that the allowance is pro-rated for the amount of time you have been in business. So if your business started on 15th March and you draw up your first set of accounts to the 31st March, you will be entitled to the following allowance:

$$£200,000 \times 16/365 = £8,767$$

For purchases over the limit you normally only get a writing-down allowance of 18%.

You should note that there is no hard and fast cut off point where expenses cease being revenue and become capital and if the tax treatment is the same then I can't see a tax inspector worrying about whether you have booked small items to an expense category or claimed the Annual Investment Allowance.

Self Employment (Full)

In the preceding chapters we have concentrated on the 'short' form which is applicable, broadly speaking, if your turnover was under £85,000 in 2017/18 and your accounting period aligns to the tax year.

For those of you with a larger business you unfortunately need the more detailed 'Self-employment (full)' form. The good news is this is just more of the same with different box numbers. I take you through the main features to look out for on the full return below.

You can download a copy of the form and notes from the HMRC website:

www.gov.uk/government/publications/self-assessment-self-employment-full-sa103f

Let's take a closer look at the various sections:

SEF1

Business details. This is largely the same as before with a few more details required, such as the name of your business.

Other information. Only box 11 "if your accounting date has changed permanently" is likely to apply to most small businesses.

Business income. This is identical to the short return as discussed in the earlier chapters.

SEF2

Business expenses. At first glance this looks a lot more detailed but in reality there are just a few more categories of expenses listed in the left hand column, and any disallowable expenses are listed in the right hand column. In practice you can simply deduct the disallowable expenses and include the net figure in the left hand column if that's easier.

SEF3

Net profit or loss. This is the same as the short return.

Tax allowances for vehicles and equipment (capital allowances). This looks rather confusing at first glance but the main boxes are box 49 for the Annual Investment Allowance, box 50 for capital allowances at 18% and box 51 for capital allowances at 8%.

The total allowances go in box 57. The other boxes are likely to apply to only a minority of businesses.

Calculating your taxable profit or loss. This is where things start to get rather more complex and this section continues onto page SEF4. The 'vanilla' entry is simply box 64 (net profit), and boxes 66 and 67 showing your "basis period" (in other words, the dates to which you have drawn up the accounts).

If you think any other boxes apply you probably need to get some professional help as a lot of the concepts here are quite complex, including where your accounts are drawn up to a different date than the tax year as you will have to fiddle about with overlap relief (boxes 68 to 70).

SEF4

Losses. Box 77 is equivalent to box 32 on the short form, i.e. the total losses computed. Boxes 78, 79 and 80 are just the same as boxes 33, 34 and 35 discussed in Chapter 12.

CIS deductions and tax taken off. Include in box 81 any CIS deductions you have suffered if you are in the CIS scheme. Put any other tax not included elsewhere in box 82. This will probably be bank interest if you have included your gross interest in box 16, rather than including it on page TR3 of the main tax return.

SEF5

Balance sheet. This section is where you put details of your business balance sheet. The important point to make here is that this page is completely voluntary! That is to say HMRC does not insist that you complete it.

There is therefore little to be gained by putting this information together.

Creating a balance sheet requires a good understanding of double entry bookkeeping and is beyond most small business owners. It's an 'optional extra' that your accountant may provide for your own management purposes but is not something you need to be concerned about when completing your tax return.

National Insurance contributions. If your total profits for 2017/18 are less than £6,025 and you choose to pay Class 2 National Insurance voluntarily, you tick box 100. If you're exempt from Class 4 National Insurance you tick box 101.

SEF6

Any other information. This can be used to give additional information where directed to do so elsewhere on the form.

The only practical use of this is to provide additional explanations to HMRC where you have unusual entries, for example a very large entry in any of the boxes.

For example, if Emily had taken £10,000 of goods for private use in box 27, rather than £200, this would be quite unusual given her turnover of £12,150 and may spark questions about the accuracy of the return. The HMRC computers use statistical analysis to spot oddities for further investigation, so it helps to have a ready explanation.

Chapter 15

General Self-Assessment Tips

- Don't leave your tax return until the last minute. If you are completing it yourself you will almost certainly find things you need to check, which could take some time.

- HMRC publishes a number of guides to help you complete your tax return. They aren't very practical but do help you with specific boxes. Have a look at the *Self-employment (short) notes*

www.gov.uk/government/publications/self-assessment-self-employment-short-sa103s

and *Self-employment (full) notes*:

www.gov.uk/government/publications/self-assessment-self-employment-full-sa103f

The following page on HMRC's website contains additional information that you may find useful:

www.gov.uk/topic/business-tax/self-employed

- Complete your return online. As long as you don't leave it until January, when the whole system tends to slow up, the online filing for self-assessment is really quite good. Not only does it add up a lot of the boxes for you, it now directs you to the parts of the return you must complete, with relevant questions and checks to see if you have made any obvious errors.

Filling in your tax return online also cuts out the risk of HMRC making keying errors when manually processing your paper return.

There is a small initial delay because you need to register for this service in advance and security codes are sent out to you. But once registered you can ensure that your return is submitted on time and find out much faster what you owe or are owed.

- Paper forms should be submitted by the end of October, and unfortunately if you have a distant memory of overpaying the tax due to avoid the fine this has long since gone. If you have missed the October deadline then you should probably try filing online.

- If you really don't know what you are doing, get some proper help. It really is a case of 'garbage in, garbage out'. It doesn't matter how beautifully you fill in the forms, if the numbers are wrong you may end up paying too much or too little tax.

With the local tax office having long since been replaced by the call centre, the quality of help available from HMRC can vary considerably. So always call twice to ensure that you get the same answer. Daft though it may seem, things really can be this hit and miss. For VAT enquiries a transcript of the conversation is made and put on your file. If it transpires that you have been misled you will tend to get an apology rather than a fine. Unfortunately with self assessment unless you have an answer in writing, all they may have is a log of the call, but not its contents.

Section 5

Accounting for Limited Companies

Chapter 16

The Basics

So far this guide has looked at the accounting and tax treatment of sole trader businesses only. There are, however, two main ways to trade in the UK: as a sole trader/partnership or through a limited company.

The main reason to trade as a sole trader is simplicity both in terms of set up and record keeping. The main reasons to trade as a limited company are added credibility, limitation of liability and some tax advantages, although these have been reduced since April 2016 due to higher taxes on dividends.

Given that many readers may at some point wish to run their business through a company, it's useful to outline the main issues. In particular, a limited company has additional reporting requirements and also requires a fundamental improvement in the quality of your accounting records.

In the first bookkeeping section we covered accounting controls and reconciliation of your business bank account. As a sole trader, any overlap between your personal money and the money of the business can be glossed over to a certain extent when completing your self-assessment tax return.

With a limited company no such short-cut can be made as the limited company and the owner/director are separate legal entities. Transactions between a company and its directors have important tax implications and directors have certain statutory legal obligations.

Chapter 17

How to Benefit from a Director's Loan Account

Going back to our very basic spreadsheets we had three tabs:

1. Sales
2. Expenses
3. Bank Account

We now add a fourth:

4. The Director's Loan Account

The purpose of the director's loan account is to track all payments between a director and the company. There are several reasons these transactions may occur.

Payments Due from Company to Director	Payments Due from Director to Company
Initial or additional capital injected into the business by the director.	Cash sums taken out of the company for personal use.
Business expenses incurred personally by the director and not reimbursed.	Sales receipts received into personal bank account or in cash.
Salaries or bonus awarded but not paid.	Personal items paid for with company money.
Dividends awarded but not paid.	

The following spreadsheet (Figure 17.1) shows an example loan account:

Figure 17.1 Example Loan Account

		Paid	Due To Director	Balance
		£	£	£
01/01/2018	Start up funding	-	1,000.00	1,000.00
02/02/2018	Expenses	-	154.75	1,154.75
01/03/2018	Salary March	300.00	300.00	1,154.75
01/04/2018	Salary April	300.00	300.00	1,154.75
01/05/2018	Salary May	-	300.00	1,454.75
25/05/2018	Payment Made	6,000.00	-	- 4,545.25
01/06/2018	Salary June	-	300.00	- 4,245.25
15/06/2018	Interim Dividend	-	5,000.00	754.75

- An initial loan of £1,000 was made to the company on the 1st of January as a start-up fund.

- A personal expense claim of £154.75 was submitted on 2nd of February, but has not been paid by the company.

- The March and April salaries were paid out immediately.

- The May salary was awarded but not paid over.

- On the 25th May a large payment of £6,000 was made to the director, but because not all the salaries had been taken and the initial loan of £1,000 was made, the account was overdrawn by only £4,545.25

- The June salary was awarded but not paid over.

- The dividend declared on the 15th June put the account back 'in the black'.

You should note that you could dispense with the transactions on 1 March and 1 April when the salary was paid out in full. I personally prefer to keep a full record of all transactions between the director and the company.

The loan account spreadsheet doesn't exist in isolation from the other tabs on your spreadsheet. Each of these transactions will also have an entry on the other sheets.

For example the start-up funding of £1,000 will appear on the banking page as a deposit into the business bank account. Similarly the expenses and salaries will all appear on the expenses spreadsheet.

It is worth noting that we tend to use the word 'expenses' to mean two slightly different things, both business expenses incurred by the business and expenses incurred by the individual director on behalf of the business.

Fundamentally every transaction will have a second entry – this is the basis of double-entry bookkeeping, which, although outside the scope of the guide, is what you are actually doing in a small way.

When reconciling your bank account you will now have all three pages to contend with – the balance in the bank will be equal to all your sales, less all your expenses less the movements on the director's loan account after accounting for unpaid invoices.

I won't go into much more detail about taking money out of a limited company, but fundamentally this account becomes the buffer between you and the company. If you keep accurate records you can use the loan account to minimise the amounts you take in taxable salary and dividends.

What tends to happen in practice is that a dividend is formally declared every three to six months. However, instead of being paid it is left on the director's loan account (as per the transaction above on 15 June) and then drawn down over the next few months, as funds are required.

There is also the ability to overdraw the director's loan account by up to £10,000 without penalty so long as the account is repaid within nine months of your company year end. You really need to sit down with your accountant to go through the correct plan for your business, as payments to directors and the repayment of loans can become quite complex.

Chapter 18

How to Claim Back Money from Your Company

Practical Aspects

In running a small limited company the aim should be to keep your affairs as simple as possible – the fewer adjusting transactions between you and the company the better. By following these four simple steps you can make your life a lot simpler:

- All sales income should be credited to the company bank account.

- No personal expenditures should be made with company money.

- Where you incur business costs with personal money (e.g., purchase items on your credit card or business mileage) a formal expense claim should be submitted.

- Do not overdraw your director's loan account by more than £10,000 at any time.

Submission of an Expense Claim

As noted above one of the important aspects of managing a limited company is controlling transactions between the directors and the company. Although you should try to get the company to pay for as many expenses as possible, you will inevitably make some business purchases with personal money.

In order to keep this as simple and as structured as possible you should put in place a simple expense claim process to deal with these transactions on a weekly or monthly basis. There is no set format you need to follow and at its most simple you can just list the expenses on a sheet of A4, staple the receipts to the back of it and treat the claim just like an invoice from a supplier.

At a slightly more sophisticated level you could treat expense claims just like a mini set of accounts, with separate columns for different types of expenses.

Let's look at an example. Let's say Richard runs a small limited company and has the following claim for expenses he has incurred personally (Figure 18.1)

Figure 18.1 Personal Expense Claim

No.	Date	Payee	Purpose	Amount	Subsis	Travel	Accom
1	06/01/2018	Paul's Café	Lunch	5.25	5.25		
2	06/01/2018	Ariva	Train to meeting	39.50		39.50	
3	07/01/2018	Trusthouse Forte	Meeting AB&Co	110.00			110.00
				-			
				154.75	5.25	39.50	110.00

Richard had a meeting with AB & Co on 6 January, resulting in a claim for lunch, a rail ticket and overnight accommodation. The total claim is £154.75. With expenses claims, it is generally advisable to state the 'purpose' of the claim to show it was a legitimate business expense. There are lots of odd rules about what you can and can't claim but generally if you genuinely incur an expense 100% for business reasons, it will be deductible.

Richard staples his invoices to the back of his claim, so he has proof of the expenses to hand.

In terms of his main bookkeeping records, Figure 18.2 shows how the entry would look as one line on his business expenses spreadsheet.

Figure 18.2 Business Expenses Spreadsheet

No.	Date	Payee	Description	Amount	Subsis	Travel	Accom
856	02/02/2018	Richard	Jan Expenses	154.75	5.25	39.50	110.00
				-			
				-			
				154.75	5.25	39.50	110.00

As you can see, we don't simply have a separate analysis column for 'personally incurred expenses', and drop the total in. Instead we split the personal expenses into the different categories.

In terms of his director's loan account, if the full amount is not paid out, then this would appear as an increase in the director's loan account.

Note that if Richard had been VAT registered we would need to know what expenses included VAT and therefore what was reclaimable by the business. For the avoidance of doubt VAT incurred by a director on behalf of a business can be reclaimed on the company VAT return in the normal way so long as proper records are kept.

Reclaiming Business Mileage

Given the high tax on most company-owned vehicles, company car ownership is becoming quite rare in small businesses. Claims for business mileage undertaken in personal vehicles are therefore increasingly common.

Generally business mileage can be claimed on journeys made for business purposes in your own car. The mileage you can claim is the *lesser* of:

- The distance from your normal place of work to your destination, or

- The distance from your start point (for example, your home) to your destination.

Where a business is based at home, your home will be classified as your normal place of work. In other words, all mileage for business purposes can be claimed.

Where business mileage is claimed, it is a requirement that each journey is listed with the following information: the date, the start point, the destination and the purpose of the visit. An example is contained in figure 18.3.

Figure 18.3 Business Mileage Log

Date	From	To	Purpose	Miles	Cost
25/4/2018	Office	Manchester	Visit Mr A Consultation	315	£141.75
26/4/2018	Office	Ipswich	Acorn Ltd, Repair	25	£11.25
			Total	340	£153.00

The rates under the 'Fixed Profit Car Scheme' for 2018/19 are 45p per mile for the first 10,000 business miles travelled during the tax year, and 25p thereafter.

This is why the total cost in the above spreadsheet is £153: 340 miles x 45p.

If you do a lot of business mileage it is therefore necessary to keep a running total (measured on a tax year basis) so you know at what point you pass the 10,000-mile threshold.

The total amount of £153 would be added to the basic expense claim as above and processed the same way.

Care should be taken to ensure that actual distances are used and not rough estimates. If in doubt use something like Google Maps, or the RAC or AA route planner to check distances:

www.google.co.uk/maps

Personally, I find it a lot easier to enter a list of postcodes into Google Maps than mess around with a notepad in the car or fiddle about with a phone app.

Tax Tip
Although VAT cannot be claimed on the full 45p, there is a VAT reclaim available for a portion that is notionally allocated to fuel. There are published rates of the 'fuel' element depending on the size of the car engine (the "Advisory Fuel Rates"), which works out to a couple of pence per mile. If you do a lot of mileage (and it's not worthwhile if you only do a few hundred) it may be worth calculating this. The current ones should be available here, with older rates linked at the bottom of the page:

www.gov.uk/government/publications/advisory-fuel-rates

Chapter 19

Limited Company Summary

The previous chapters provide a brief overview of some of the extra record keeping requirements for companies. If you endeavour to keep your business and your personal finances as separate as possible you shouldn't run into too many problems with your bookkeeping.

Finally, I'm leaving this section with a short plea – if you are running a limited company please get yourself an accountant at the earliest opportunity. This isn't a desperate measure to drum up business for my profession. It comes from frustration at seeing decent hardworking people getting very stressed and spending a lot of time trying to deal with and submit their own limited company accounts – often with expensive consequences in terms of late filing fees and poor practices.

Fundamentally, if your business is big enough to have incorporated, it should be big enough to allow for a few hundred pounds in professional fees to get things sorted out properly. In most cases the fees are easily recovered once all the proper tax planning is put in place to utilise the tax breaks available to you.

Section 6

Everything You Need to Know About VAT

Chapter 20

Basic Bookkeeping with VAT

In the pages that follow we'll look at how to practically set out your records if you need to account for VAT and how to complete your quarterly VAT return.

This section builds on the earlier bookkeeping chapters. If you are diving straight in here, it may be helpful to read through the earlier sections to familiarise yourself with the spreadsheet formats I use in the examples.

Sales Spreadsheet

Let's kick off with a simple example of sales income for a service business. Here's how the information is recorded on the sales spreadsheet (Figure 20.1)

Figure 20.1 Sales Spreadsheet Including VAT

Ref	Description	Date	Net	VAT	Gross	Date Paid
INV001	Mr A	05/01/2018	1,000.00	200.00	1,200.00	23/01/2018
INV002	Mr C	06/01/2018	250.00	50.00	300.00	
Total			1,250.00	250.00	1,500.00	

- 'Ref' is the sequential and unique invoice number
- 'Description' is the client's name and perhaps the work completed
- 'Date' is the invoice date
- 'Net' is the pre-VAT cost
- 'VAT' is the VAT charge
- 'Gross' is the VAT-inclusive figure billed to the client
- 'Date paid' the date the payment cleared in the business bank account

This is identical to the very first example given in Chapter 1, except that the totals are split into Net, VAT and Gross.

Furthermore, a 'Date Paid' column has been added, the use of which will become apparent shortly.

Net vs Gross

It is helpful at this point to remind yourself what net and gross mean in practical terms.

- 'Net' is the amount that you actually earn – this is the number that will appear in your accounts as turnover.

- 'VAT' is the amount of tax that you will eventually pay over to HM Revenue and Customs.

- 'Gross' is the total amount of the invoice you are sending out, and the amount of actual money you are going to be paid by your customer.

Excel Tip - Make the Formulas do the Hard Work

When using spreadsheets, it makes a lot of sense to calculate the VAT due using a formula as this will save a lot of pointless data entry.

Emily, who sells art to the general public, may sell an item for £200 inclusive of VAT. She will then need to work out the VAT from this total gross sales price.

Someone else selling professional services will tend to quote a fee such as £100 + VAT.

Emily will enter the £200 in the gross column on her spreadsheet and set up two formulas:

- Net = Gross / 1.2
- VAT = Gross – Net

Someone selling professional services will enter the £100 in the net column and set up two similar formulas:

- VAT = Net * 0.2
- Gross = Net + VAT

Taxcafe has a useful VAT calculator that does these calculations for you. It is available free from:

www.taxcafe.co.uk/vatcalc

Expenses Spreadsheet

Now we have dealt with the income, the expenses should be relatively straightforward. The basic layout below (Figure 20.2) is much the same as in the original example in Chapter 1:

Figure 20.2 Expenses Spreadsheet Including VAT

No.	Date	Payee	Description	Gross	VAT	Net	Stationery	Books	Drawings
1	05/01/2018	Staples	Office Supplies	59.50	9.92	49.58	49.58		
2	06/01/2018	Taxcafe	Books	24.95	-	24.95		24.95	
3	22/01/2018	Self	Drawings	105.00	-	105.00			105.00
				189.45	9.92	179.53	49.58	24.95	105.00

- 'Net' is the pre-VAT cost
- 'VAT' is the VAT charge
- 'Gross' is the VAT-inclusive figure that you physically pay

You should note one important item here – the analysis columns are based on the *net* of VAT figures, rather than the gross figures. This is important because when it comes to drawing up your accounts it is these after-VAT figures we are interested in.

Unfortunately, it's common for accountants to have to point this out to clients *after* all the numbers have been done, resulting in a big editing exercise.

You can see in this example that only one item, 'office supplies', actually carries any VAT. Books are free from VAT and drawings are outside the scope of VAT. You, therefore, need to be careful only to include VAT on items on which you have definitely been charged VAT.

If in doubt ask your supplier for a VAT invoice that clearly shows the VAT charge.

Overseas Issues

You have to provide information of purchases and sales made outside the UK on your VAT return. This applies to even the smallest VAT-registered business buying or selling overseas.

I generally recommend the inclusion of an extra column on your spreadsheets denoting the origin of the purchase or sale as 'UK', 'EU' or 'W' for worldwide.

Remember that EU VAT is not directly reclaimable on your UK VAT return and therefore European invoices are effectively treated as if the invoice has come from a non-VAT registered supplier in the UK, with no entry in the VAT column.

Figure 20.3 below shows a typical layout (the analysis columns have been dropped for simplicity).

Figure 20.3 Expenses Spreadsheet Including Overseas Purchases

No.	Date	Payee	Description	Origin	Gross	VAT	Net	Analysis
1	05/01/2018	Staples	Office Supplies	UK	59.50	9.92	49.58	
2	06/01/2018	Taxcafe	Books	UK	24.95	-	24.95	
3	22/01/2018	Irish Ltd	Stock	EU	252.00	-	252.00	
4	28/01/2018	USA Inc	Stock	W	500.00	83.33	416.67	
					836.45	93.25	743.20	

Note the new column, 'Origin', denoting the source of the purchases.

- The first purchase from Staples is from the UK with full UK VAT applied.

- The second transaction, also from the UK, has no entry as there is no VAT on books.

- The third purchase from Irish Ltd (based in Ireland) is from the EU. Irish VAT was not charged because the UK VAT number was provided to Irish Ltd to avoid it being added in the first place.

- The fourth purchase of stock from the US also carries VAT. VAT on goods imported from non-EU countries is normally charged at the same rate as if the goods were purchased in the UK. You can reclaim this VAT as input tax if you have the import VAT certificate (form C79) showing that you have paid the import VAT.

The same columns would also be required on the sales spreadsheet if you sell to overseas customers, as seen in Figure 20.4.

Figure 20.4 Sales Spreadsheet Including Overseas Sales

Ref	Description	Date	Origin	Net	VAT	Gross	Date Paid
INV001	Mr A	05/01/2018	UK	1,000.00	200.00	1,200.00	23/01/2018
INV002	Mr C	06/01/2018	EU	250.00	50.00	300.00	
INV003	Mr X	07/01/2018	EU	500.00	-	500.00	
INV004	Mr Z	20/01/2018	W	800.00	-	800.00	
Total				2,550.00	250.00	2,800.00	

- The first sale to Mr A is a straightforward sale for £1,000 plus VAT.

- The sale to Mr C carried VAT even through Mr C is in the EU. This is because Mr C is a private individual. You are generally obliged to charge VAT to other persons in the EU unless they are VAT-registered businesses.

- Mr X is also in the EU, but being a VAT registered business in France and having supplied a valid VAT number he is not charged VAT. Had Mr X not provided a French VAT number, VAT would have to be included on this invoice, just like it was for Mr C.

- Mr Z is based in the US and has no VAT added under any circumstances, as VAT only applies to sales within the EU.

If this is a bit confusing, it will help to go back to Chapter 6 and have a look again at the overseas issues.

This sort of formatting works if you have a small number of overseas transactions (or indeed only a small number of UK ones).

If you have lots of transactions from all over the world (now quite common with website businesses), things might get more complicated, especially if you have digital sales and the new rules outlined in Chapter 6 apply.

You could perhaps keep a separate list of purchases and sales from the UK, EU and US by using separate spreadsheets, or it might be time to look at an accounting software package.

Chapter 21

How to Complete Your VAT Return

Even if you don't plan to complete your own VAT returns, it's definitely worth knowing how to do them. This way you will understand what information you need to collect on your spreadsheets and pass over to your accountant.

Let's look first at the layout of a VAT return and what data is required (see below). The first thing to note is that the VAT return is extremely short, with just nine boxes:

VAT due in this period on **sales** and other outputs (Box 1): £

VAT due in this period on **acquisitions** from other **EC Member States** (Box 2): £

Total VAT due **(the sum of boxes 1 and 2)** (Box 3): £

VAT reclaimed in this period on **purchases** and other inputs, (including acquisitions from the EC) (Box 4): £

Net VAT to be paid to HM Revenue & Customs or reclaimed by you **(Difference between boxes 3 and 4)** (Box 5): £

Total value of **sales** and all other outputs excluding any VAT. **Include your box 8 figure** (Box 6): £

Total value of **purchases** and all other inputs excluding any VAT. **Include your box 9 figure** (Box 7): £

Total value of all **supplies** of goods and related costs, excluding any VAT, to other **EC Member States** (Box 8): £

Total value of all **acquisitions** of goods and related costs, excluding any VAT, from other **EC Member States** (Box 9): £

Methods of Filing

HMRC has required all VAT-registered businesses to file their VAT returns online since April 2012. Therefore if you are reading this book as a refresher, having completed VAT returns in the past, those green forms you may remember are no more.

There are two basic methods of filing:

1. Using HMRC's online service
2. Using a link from your own accounting software

HMRC's online service is fairly good and suitable for most small businesses:

www.gov.uk/vat-returns/send-your-return

Most major accounting packages now offer the facility to file your VAT return directly from the software. The main advantage of this is that you don't have to re-key your figures which will of course reduce the risk of error. However, there is always a danger with software of "garbage in, garbage out". In particular, software rarely seems to get boxes 6 to 9 right, with data such as payroll, which is outside the scope of VAT, often ending up recorded as an expense when it shouldn't be. Therefore it is important that all the boxes are checked carefully rather than just hitting "send" and hoping for the best!

> **Tip:** The VAT system has a direct debit payment option which is helpful for two reasons. Firstly, you do not have to worry about forgetting to pay. Secondly, the direct debit payments come out of your account on the 10th of the month (or later if a weekend). This gives you at least three days longer than the bank transfer deadline and there is no need to allow a few extra days for the payment to arrive either.

Changes to VAT Filing

As part of HMRC's "Making Tax Digital" programme, there is a proposed change to the way VAT returns are filed.

This is due to start from April 2019 and requires businesses to use new third party software to create a 'digital link' between their record keeping and the filing software, instead of keying the figures directly onto HMRC's online VAT form.

If you are already using third party accounting software with a VAT filing functionality, I imagine you will not really notice the difference.

However, if you are completing accounts in Excel or legacy desktop software and using HMRC's portal to file, this represents a significant change.

At the time of writing (June 2018) there was no third party software available to small businesses. The pilot is open to only a very limited number of users and most of HMRC's development resources are consumed by Brexit issues. It seems more than possible the April 2019 deadline will be extended for a further 12 months until April 2020.

All I can say right now is that you should be aware of this issue and, if it goes ahead, I understand HMRC is poised to send out a letter to all VAT registered businesses. Do however check carefully at the time if it voluntary or not. I can't see any specific advantage for taxpayers in using the new method.

> **Tip:** If you are voluntarily registered for VAT (that is to say your turnover is below the VAT threshold, but have chosen to register) the draft rules suggest you can use the current system and so avoid the inevitable cost of purchasing third party software.

Basic VAT Return Example

Let's start with a straightforward example of a VAT-registered business with no international purchases or sales. I have listed all the boxes on the VAT return in Figure 21.1. Only the un-shaded boxes are relevant to this example. The shaded boxes deal with sales and purchases of goods to and from EC member states.

Figure 21.1 VAT Return Boxes

Box	Wording on the VAT Return	What This Means in Plain English
1	VAT due in this period on sales and other outputs.	The total VAT on your sales. Your output VAT
2	VAT due in this period on acquisitions from other EC Member States	Not applicable
3	Total VAT due (sum of boxes 1 and 2)	Add 1 and 2 together
4	VAT reclaimed in this period on purchases and other inputs (including acquisitions from the EC)	The total VAT on your costs. Your input VAT
5	Net VAT to be paid to HM Revenue & Customs or reclaimed by you (Difference between boxes 3 and 4)	Box 3 minus Box 4
6	Total value of sales and all other outputs excluding any VAT. Include your Box 8 figure	Your sales before adding VAT
7	Total value of purchases and all other inputs excluding any VAT. Include your Box 9 figure	Your expenses before adding VAT
8	Total value of all supplies of goods and related costs, excluding any VAT, to other EC Member States	Not applicable
9	Total value of all acquisitions of goods and related costs, excluding any VAT, from other EC Member States	Not applicable

So what we need to come up with is:

- The total VAT on your sales (box 1)
- The total VAT on your costs (box 4)
- Your sales before adding VAT (box 6)
- Your expenses before adding VAT (box 7)

Using the basic sales information contained in Figure 21.2, we can quickly find the right data to include on the VAT return.

Figure 21.2 Sales Data

Ref	Description	Date	Net	VAT	Gross	Date Paid
INV001	Mr A	05/01/2018	1,000.00	200.00	1,200.00	23/01/2018
INV002	Mr C	06/01/2018	250.00	50.00	300.00	
Total			1,250.00	250.00	1,500.00	

We can see that the total output VAT (VAT on sales) is £250. This number goes in box 1 on the VAT return. The total net sales (sales excluding VAT) are £1,250. This number goes in box 6.

Excel Tip

We can also check that the figures are correct by multiplying net sales by the current VAT rate (20%):

£1,250 * 0.2 = £250

Now this may seem a little farcical when dealing with just two transactions, but if you have 500 (or even 50) sales in the period it makes a lot of sense to double check the figures in this way. If we know that all sales carry VAT this figure should be identical every time.

In practice some sales may not carry VAT. But if your spreadsheet is telling you that the total VAT on your sales is £520, and the total net sales are £1,250 you would quickly see that this is more than the maximum possible VAT (£250). You would therefore hopefully spot the transposition error of the '2' and the '5'. This type of sanity check is good practice.

Expenses

Figure 21.3 Expenses Data

Date	Payee	Description	Gross	VAT	Net	Stationery	Books	Drawings	Insurance
05/01/2018	Staples	Office Supplies	59.50	9.92	49.58	49.58			
06/01/2018	Taxcafe	Books	24.95	-	24.95		24.95		
22/01/2018	Self	Drawings	105.00	-	105.00			105.00	
			189.45	9.92	179.53	49.58	24.95	105.00	0

The total VAT on costs (also known as input VAT) is £9.92 and goes in box 4 of the VAT return. Note there is no VAT on books and no VAT on money drawn out of the business (although drawings do feature in your records as an 'expense').

The figure used for total expenses before VAT (your net purchases) is not £179.53. We need to take off the drawings of £105, which leaves us with £74.53. This is the number that goes in box 7 of the VAT return.

Apart from drawings, other transactions that are outside the scope of VAT include bank interest, dividends and changes to directors' loan accounts, if the business is a limited company.

It is worth noting that even if you had included drawings by accident it wouldn't actually affect the amount of VAT you have to pay over to HMRC.

Your first VAT return (apart from my shading) will now look something like Figure 21.4

Figure 21.4 Completing the Basic VAT Return

Box No.	Description	£	p
1	VAT due in this period on sales and other outputs.	250	00
2	n/a	0	00
3	Total VAT due (the sum of boxes 1 and 2)	250	00
4	VAT reclaimed in this period on purchases and other inputs (including acquisitions from the EC)	9	92
5	Net VAT to be paid to HM Revenue & Customs or reclaimed by you (Difference between boxes 3 and 4)	240	08
6	Total value of sales and all other outputs excluding any VAT. Include your Box 8 figure	1,250	00
7	Total value of purchases and all other inputs excluding any VAT. Include your Box 9 figure	74	00
8	n/a	0	00
9	n/a	0	00

The total VAT payable to HMRC is contained in box 5: £240.08.

Note the following:

- Where there are no figures to include (as in boxes 2, 8 and 9) you will still need to enter a zero on the online return.

- Boxes 1-5 are completed using pounds and pence. Boxes 6-9 are completed using pounds only. Note that HMRC doesn't use proper mathematical rounding but simply truncates the figures and ignores the pence. So it would be £74 in box 7 regardless of whether the expenses happened to be £74.43 or £74.53. Most people would assume £74.53 would become £75, rounding up to the nearest pound. But not HMRC. They would still expect £74! In practice it would take a rather pedantic tax inspector to get upset about such details but it always helps to make it look as if you know what you are doing when it's your turn for a VAT inspection.

The Importance of Timing

VAT returns are generally produced on a quarterly basis – once every three months.

You have to make sure you include the right invoices in the right VAT period. If you are using the accruals basis it's the date on the invoice that usually matters, not the date when payment is actually made.

For example, if your VAT period runs from January to March you have to include all sales and expense invoices that are dated January to March.

Some readers may be wondering whether they can manipulate their invoice dates to push VAT payments into later periods. Unfortunately HMRC is, as ever, one step ahead and has introduced something called a 'basic tax point'. What this means is they look at the underlying transaction to ensure you are not pushing things too hard.

For businesses with trading stock the relevant date is quite clear cut – it is the date on which the stock physically leaves your premises. For service businesses things get a bit more complicated but the 'basic tax point' is when you have completed the service.

You are allowed 14 days from this 'basic tax point' to get your invoice out, and the rules state that so long as you issue an invoice within 14 days, the 'tax point' is indeed the invoice date. If you haven't managed it within 14 days then the 'basic tax point' takes precedent.

Let's take a look at an example to clarify some of the points discussed so far.

Example

Margaret is a landscape gardener. Her current VAT return covers the three months from May to July. In July she has completed three jobs:

- *Harry – £200 for work carried out from 27 June to 5 July.*
- *Dolly – £300 for work carried out from 10 July to 18 July.*
- *An ongoing job for Helen at £500 per month, with invoices sent out at the end of each month.*

Now if Margaret sends out invoices at the end of the month for all three jobs her VAT payment will be £120.00 (£1,000 x 20%). This is the current VAT rate.

If she sends out her invoices on 1 August she may decide to include all three amounts in her next VAT return, covering the period August to October. However, this isn't quite right. Harry's invoice for £200+VAT (£240) relates to work completed on 5 July, so the tax point is in July. The £40 VAT is therefore still due with the current VAT return, even though the invoice hasn't been sent out.

Dolly's invoice can be included in the next VAT period because there are fewer than 14 days between completing the job and sending out the invoice on August 1. This sort of adjustment makes things all a bit too complicated for Margaret's liking (she wants to be out designing gardens not worrying about VAT), so she vows to invoice everything within the month to keep it simple.

Margaret is, however, missing a trick. The ongoing job for Helen of £500 per month could actually be billed on 1 August, instead of 31 July, thereby deferring £100 of VAT to the next quarter.

If you do bill a lot of work on the last day of the month it can make a lot of sense to bill on the first day of the new month. However, you mustn't lose sight of the fact that we are only talking about *deferring* your VAT payments for three months, not avoiding the tax altogether. Most small businesses are more concerned about getting paid as quickly as possible rather than postponing their VAT payments.

Tips to Keep Your VAT Returns Simple

- Always send out your invoices on the same day you complete a job or send out goods. This is good for cash flow too!
- If you must wait until the end of the month to send out your invoices, make sure they are dated the current month and not the next month.
- For ongoing work, wait until the first day of the new month rather than the end of the old one.

If you follow this set of rules you won't have to think about it too much and will have more time to spend on your business.

Chapter 22

Overseas Purchases & Sales

It's time to look at a more complex VAT return with overseas purchases and sales.

Figure 22.1 VAT Return Boxes

Box	Wording on the VAT Return	What This Means in Plain English
1	VAT due in this period on sales and other outputs.	The total VAT on your sales. Your output VAT
2	VAT due in this period on acquisitions from other EC Member States	n/a to most businesses
3	Total VAT due (sum of boxes 1 and 2)	Add 1 and 2 together
4	VAT reclaimed in this period on purchases and other inputs (including acquisitions from the EC)	The total VAT on your costs. Your input VAT
5	Net VAT to be paid to HM Revenue & Customs or reclaimed by you (Difference between boxes 3 and 4)	Box 3 minus Box 4
6	Total value of sales and all other outputs excluding any VAT. Include your Box 8 figure	Your sales before adding VAT
7	Total value of purchases and all other inputs excluding any VAT. Include your Box 9 figure	Your expenses before adding VAT
8	Total value of all supplies of goods and related costs, excluding any VAT, to other EC Member States	Generally sales to VAT registered EU customers only
9	Total value of all acquisitions of goods and related costs, excluding any VAT, from other EC Member States	Purchases from VAT registered suppliers in the EU

Boxes 8 and 9 are now filled in, although I am going to ignore box 2 as it seldom applies to most UK businesses. This box is used if you import from the EU but haven't yet paid for the goods or services. It's a bit complex but all you need to know is that in the worst case scenario you will end up with a timing difference (i.e. payment of VAT in the wrong period) rather than a total underpayment of VAT.

If your business is small enough to have manual records you probably don't have to worry about this point unless an inspector has told you otherwise.

So this time around we need to know a bit more detail:

- The total VAT on your sales (Box 1)
- The total VAT on your costs (Box 4)
- Your sales before adding VAT (Box 6)
- Your expenses before adding VAT (Box 7)
- Net sales to VAT-registered EU customers (Box 8)
- Net purchases from VAT-registered EU suppliers (Box 9)

You may like to note that the figures for boxes 8 and 9 are also included within the totals for boxes 6 and 7. A summary of the sales is contained in Figure 22.2:

Figure 22.2 Sales Spreadsheet Including Overseas Sales

Ref	Description	Date	Origin	Net	VAT	Gross	Date Paid
INV001	Mr A	05/01/2018	UK	1,000.00	200.00	1,200.00	23/01/2018
INV002	Mr C	06/01/2018	EU	250.00	50.00	300.00	
INV003	Mr X	07/01/2018	EU	500.00	-	500.00	
INV004	Mr Z	20/01/2018	W	800.00	-	800.00	
Total				2,550.00	250.00	2,800.00	

Total output VAT (box 1) is again quite straightforward being the total of the VAT column: £250. The total sales before adding VAT (box 6) are also quite easy to find – the total of the net sales column: £2,550.

To get to the total net sales within the EU (box 8) we need to add up each sale with an 'EU' in the Origin column. However, you should filter out customers who are not VAT registered (e.g. private individuals) where you have not exceeded the country's 'distance selling' threshold. Each EU country has its own distance selling threshold (e.g. €35,000). In this case there is one transaction to a VAT registered customer in the EU: Mr X. Thus the total included in box 8 is £500.

A summary of the expenses is contained in Figure 22.3.

Figure 22.3 Expenses Spreadsheet Including Overseas Purchases

No.	Date	Payee	Description	Origin	Gross	VAT	Net	Analysis
1	05/01/2018	Staples	Office Supplies	UK	59.50	9.92	49.58	
2	06/01/2018	Taxcafe	Books	UK	24.95	-	24.95	
3	22/01/2018	Irish Ltd	Stock	EU	252.00	-	252.00	
4	28/01/2018	USA Inc	Stock	W	500.00	83.33	416.67	
					836.45	93.25	743.20	

In this example the total VAT on costs (the input VAT) is £93.25 and goes in box 4 on the VAT return. The total expenses before VAT (net purchases) are £743.20 and go in box 7. There are no adjustments in this example for items outside the scope of VAT.

In box 9 you enter the total value of goods you received from VAT registered suppliers in other EU countries. In this example the net purchases from the EU are £252.

The final VAT return looks like this:

Figure 22.4 Completing the VAT Return, Overseas Transactions

Box	Description	£	p
1	VAT due in this period on sales and other outputs	250	00
2	VAT due in this period on acquisitions from other EC Member States	0	00
3	Total VAT due (the sum of boxes 1 and 2)	250	00
4	VAT reclaimed in this period on purchases and other inputs (including acquisitions from the EC)	93	25
5	Net VAT to be paid to HM Revenue & Customs or reclaimed by you (Difference between boxes 3 and 4)	156	75
6	Total value of sales and all other outputs excluding any VAT. Include your box 8 figure	2,550	00
7	Total values of purchases and all other inputs excluding any VAT. Include your box 9 figure	743	20
8	Total value of all supplies of goods and related costs, excluding any VAT, to other EC Member States	500	00
9	Total value of all acquisitions of goods and related costs, excluding any VAT, from other EC Member States	252	00

Now this may all seem rather complex at first glance but if you work through the numbers a couple of times you should see that, if you record your income and expenses correctly, producing your own VAT return isn't all that difficult once you know how.

For further help, HMRC runs quite good free courses for new business owners to help them get to grips with VAT and other aspects of tax.

If you can manage to set aside the time, a half or full day's training may be worthwhile.

Excel Tip

In these simple examples it has been easy to work out the EU figures. In practice it is probably somewhat more difficult. When preparing VAT returns for clients from their spreadsheets, I tend to copy the relevant data into a separate spreadsheet and use the Excel 'sort' function so all the UK, EU and W sales appear together. I can then easily total up the UK, EU and worldwide data. When carrying out 'sorts' it is always important to double check the total of the original data with the totals on the sorted data or it is easy to make a mistake.

Chapter 23

Pros & Cons of the Cash Basis

The cash basis for VAT is available to many smaller businesses. Rather than include income and expenses within your VAT return on the date an invoice is sent out or received, transactions are only included when payment is received or made. This is clearly of considerable advantage where a business has a lot of sales invoices that are only paid after a considerable time lag.

However, using the cash basis can make completing your VAT return a lot tougher, as the date of payment rather than the date on the invoice becomes important.

Let's look again at the sales records in the example we have been using:

Figure 23.1 Sales Spreadsheet

Ref	Description	Date	Net	VAT	Gross	Date Paid
INV001	Mr A	05/01/2018	1,000.00	200.00	1,200.00	23/01/2018
INV002	Mr C	06/01/2018	250.00	50.00	300.00	
Total			1,250.00	250.00	1,500.00	

On the right is the 'Date Paid' column. If we can account on a cash basis this becomes crucial, as only items for which payment has been received are included. Without re-working another VAT return we can quickly see that under cash accounting in this period we don't yet have to pay over the VAT on invoice 002 of £50, which represents a small but real cash flow advantage.

So far so good but in practice things get a bit harder once you have lots of transactions.

The main problem is that rather than being able to 'draw a line' between each accounting period and add up the data, you find yourself having to add up on a line-by-line basis the income and expenses that have come in or gone out between certain dates.

I like to follow a similar process to that outlined for determining whether sales are inside or outside the EU and UK and copy the data into a separate spreadsheet and sort by the 'paid date'. This is fine in theory but in practice the more manipulation you do, the greater the chance of error or omission.

As a rule of thumb I wouldn't generally suggest you persevere with cash accounting using spreadsheet software. If your cash flow is tight enough to make cash flow accounting worthwhile I would seriously consider the use of a basic accounting package that will do all these computations for you.

Otherwise your VAT return will turn into a quarterly hair-pulling exercise when instead you could concentrate on collecting some of these old debts.

Chapter 24

How to Benefit from the Flat Rate Scheme

In contrast to cash accounting, accounting within the flat rate scheme is pretty straightforward.

As you probably know, the 'standard' VAT rate is 20%. Under the flat rate scheme the tax rate applied to your sales when completing your VAT return is lower, so you have less output tax to pay HMRC. The flip side is that you are not allowed to claim back any input tax on your expenses.

Different businesses are allowed to use different tax rates, designed to leave them neither better off nor out of pocket using the system (although, of course, all businesses are different so some will be better off financially and some will be worse off financially). All businesses that use the flat rate scheme do, however, benefit from having a simplified VAT return.

Let's return to our familiar sales spreadsheet and assume that the business is allowed to use a VAT rate of 12% under the flat rate scheme:

Figure 24.1 Sales Spreadsheet

Ref	Description	Date	Net	VAT	Gross	Date Paid
INV001	Mr A	05/01/2018	1,000.00	200.00	1,200.00	23/01/2018
INV002	Mr C	06/01/2018	250.00	50.00	300.00	
Total			1,250.00	250.00	1,500.00	

You'll notice that the VAT rate used on the invoices is still 20%. In other words, when you send out invoices to your customers you still use the 20% rate as normal. The 12% rate is only used when completing the VAT return.

If this business is on the 12% scheme, we simply take 12% of the GROSS sales:

£1,500 x 0.12 = £180.00

This is the amount of tax paid over to HMRC.

You'll notice that this is less than the £250.00 output tax appearing on the spreadsheet. However, it doesn't mean that this is a saving because no VAT can be recovered on any of the expenses of the business.

The difference between the £250.00 VAT charged on your invoices and £180.00 paid over is £70.00. This amount does unfortunately become part of your profit for tax purposes. In accounting terms it will be reported within your turnover figures.

The next change is what happens to the expenses spreadsheet. As you can see below we now totally ignore VAT and analyse the expenses on a gross basis, just as we did before VAT was included in the examples.

Figure 24.2 Expenses Spreadsheet

No.	Date	Payee	Description	Amount	Stationery	Books	Drawings
1	05/01/2018	Staples	Office Supplies	59.50	59.50		
2	06/01/2018	Taxcafe	Books	24.95		24.95	
3	22/01/2018	Self	Drawings	105.00			105.00
				-			
				-			
				189.45	59.50	24.95	105.00

This change does, of course, make your accounting easier.

The revised VAT return will look like the one in Figure 24.3. We simply show the VAT due in boxes 1, 3 and 5. There is no reclaim in box 4, nor any expenses shown in box 7.

Oddly, box 6 showing total sales, which normally contains net sales excluding VAT, contains *gross* figures. In other words it shows the total £1,500 you have invoiced your client, instead of £1,250.

Figure 24.3 Completing the VAT Return – Flat Rate Scheme

Box	Description	£	p
1	VAT due in this period on sales and other outputs	180	00
2	n/a	0	00
3	Total VAT due (the sum of boxes 1 and 2)	180	00
4	VAT reclaimed in this period on purchases and other inputs (including acquisitions from the EC)	0	00
5	Net VAT to be paid to HM Revenue & Customs or reclaimed by you (Difference between boxes 3 and 4)	180	00
6	Total value of sales and all other outputs excluding any VAT. Include your box 8 figure	1,500	00
7	Total values of purchases and all other inputs excluding any VAT. Include your box 9 figure	0	00
8	n/a	0	00
9	n/a	0	00

In this example the VAT due under the flat rate scheme is £180.00 compared with £250.00 due under the normal scheme. This is clearly a tax saving. Whether the flat rate scheme is right for *your* business is discussed in more detail in *Section 7 – How to Pay Less VAT*. In particular, since April 2017 eligibility for the scheme has become very restricted for service sector businesses.

Section 7

How to Pay Less VAT

So far in this book we have only considered the fact that either a business is VAT registered or it is not. For many small businesses the decision about whether or not to register is an important one. The aim of this section is to introduce you to some of the factors that can help you decide whether or not to register. We then go on to look at how to register for VAT and what special scheme options are available to you to make the accounting for VAT easier, and in some cases more profitable.

Chapter 25

Who Should Register for VAT Early

VAT registration is compulsory for some firms and optional for the rest.

Compulsory Registration

You probably know that compulsory registration applies if your annual turnover exceeds the VAT threshold, which has been £85,000 since April 2017. The basic rules are that you must register if either:

- At the end of any month your turnover in the last 12 months is more than £85,000.

- Your turnover is expected to exceed £85,000 in the next 30 days.

It is also possible to breach the threshold and not have to register, if you have a large 'blip' in your sales.

You can also deregister if you expect your turnover in the next 12 months to be less than £83,000.

You have 30 days to register after the threshold is reached.

You will then be registered from the first day of the second month after the month in which the threshold is reached. In plain English this means that if you hit the threshold in November, you have to register by the 30th December and start charging VAT from the 1st of January.

Please note this is a general summary, and there are quite a number of related rules and regulations that apply in some cases.

Voluntary Registration

You may choose to register for VAT even if your turnover is below the threshold. There are several reasons why you may wish to do this:

- **Credibility**. By registering for VAT you may look like a larger business than you really are. This can sometimes be helpful in winning customers in the early days.

- **Cash savings**. You will be able to recover all the VAT on your expenses (but read the comments below).

Generally speaking, if most of your clients are VAT-registered it makes sense for you to register too. Your customers won't mind having to pay VAT because they can recover it when they submit their VAT returns. You, on the other hand, will benefit from being able to claim back all the VAT you pay on your expenses.

If most of your customers are <u>not</u> registered then it may make sense to remain unregistered as long as possible. By charging VAT to unregistered customers you are effectively raising your prices, which may not be possible if you're in a price-sensitive sector.

If you register for VAT and your customers are not prepared to pay higher prices you will have to absorb the cost personally.

Let's look at some examples to see why the above statements apply.

Example 1 - VAT Registered Customer

Helen sells furniture to large businesses. She buys from VAT-registered suppliers and sells to other VAT-registered suppliers.

Let's look at a single transaction. Helen buys the furniture for £500 + VAT and sells it for £750 + VAT.

Helen's profit is simply £750 less £500 = £250.

Her VAT-registered customer is not concerned about paying £750 from a non-VAT registered company or £750 plus VAT because any VAT will be claimed back.

Had Helen not been VAT-registered her cost would have been the full VAT-inclusive price paid:

$$£500 + 20\% = £600$$

And her profit would be:

$$£750 - £600 = £150$$

This compares with profits of £250 if she is VAT-registered.

Alternatively, to keep her profits at £250, she could consider raising the price to £850. This is fine if customers are not sensitive to such increases but would normally result in less furniture being sold.

Helen concludes that, despite the extra paperwork, she is better off registering for VAT. She will also be able to reclaim VAT on office expenses and other business expenses as an added bonus.

Where most of your customers are not VAT-registered it's often better not to register voluntarily.

Example 2 – Non-VAT-Registered Customer

Helen's sister Sarah also buys furniture from a VAT-registered supplier but sells to private individuals rather than other VAT-registered businesses. She has seen how being VAT-registered increases her sister's profits and wonders if she could benefit in the same way too.

She buys the same item of furniture for £500 plus VAT, and wants to sell this for £900 to the end consumer.

If she registers for VAT she will recover the VAT on the purchase price and pay over the VAT on the sale. She works out the VAT on the selling price as follows:

Net Price	£750.00
VAT	£150.00
Gross Selling Price	£900.00

So as a VAT-registered trader she will sell at £750 and buy at £500 which results in a profit of £250. This sounds pretty good to Sarah and is equivalent to her sister's profit.

However, it could be even better if she wasn't VAT-registered. Her customers (the public) don't care if they pay £750 plus £150 VAT or just pay £900 with no VAT as it will cost them the same either way.

So if Sarah was unregistered selling at £900 she would pay costs of £600 on her purchase (£500 plus VAT) and therefore make a profit of £300. Sarah therefore makes the opposite choice to her sister, making an extra £50 per sale, which is very welcome to her in the early days of her business.

Mixed Customer Base

Where a business deals mainly with VAT registered customers, registration tends to make sense, and where you deal mainly with the public, not registering tends to be favourable.

In the real world most businesses aren't usually so neatly compartmentalised, so this section is aimed at helping you work out what is best for you. If you get stuck, your accountant or business adviser can probably help you decide. The diagram below attempts to describe the decision-making process graphically.

Figure 25.1 The VAT Registration Decision

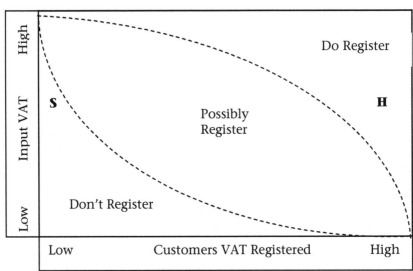

On the left is the input VAT of the business – the amount of VAT paid on expenses. The more expenses the business has, the more likely it will want to register to recover this money.

A small business providing *services*, such as a freelance journalist, accountant or consultant, will probably have very little input tax as there are probably few expenses that have VAT other than office equipment and some office supplies.

For example, for every £100 of sales there might only be £5 of costs that include VAT.

On the other hand, a business selling *products,* especially products with very low profit margins, will have high input VAT. For example, someone buying computer equipment for £90 and selling it for £100 will probably benefit more by registering for VAT.

On the bottom of the diagram we have the proportion of VAT-registered customers from Low to High, with low meaning most customers are unregistered.

The more VAT-registered customers there are, the more the business is going to benefit from registering because the customers will not mind having VAT added to their bills.

Let's look at where Helen and Sarah from the previous examples fit into the diagram.

All of Helen's customers are VAT-registered and her input VAT is medium to high. I say 'medium to high' because the purchase price of her products accounts for two-thirds of the sale price. She would appear roughly where the 'H' is marked on the diagram, implying that she should register for VAT.

None of Sarah's customers are VAT-registered but her input VAT is also medium to high, just like Helen's. Sarah would be over at the other side where the 'S' is marked, implying that she should not register for VAT.

In summary, looking at each segment separated by the dotted lines, in the left-hand segment we generally don't register where the proportion of VAT-registered customers is low and the input VAT is low. In the top right-hand segment the opposite is true.

In the middle we have a large segment where it is unclear what the best course of action is and a little more analysis is required.

Now if you are still following this (and I appreciate that clearing out the gutters may suddenly seem very appealing) I would like to explain why the proportion of input VAT is a factor.

Do you remember Tom from our basic VAT example in Chapter 5? Last time we looked in on Tom he was chopping down trees and selling them to Dick.

Tom has very little input VAT. Apart from his chainsaw and a few other bits and pieces he has very few expenses that carry VAT. Tom would be in a similar position if he was providing pretty much any service with low costs, instead of selling products.

Now instead of selling all his timber to Dick who is VAT-registered, Tom starts selling half his output to the general public. Private individuals, not being VAT-registered, are just interested in the total price including VAT.

Let's say that during the year Tom sells £30,000 made up as follows:

- £15,000 to Dick plus £3,000 VAT
- £15,000 to the public plus £3,000 VAT
- Total sales £30,000 plus £6,000 VAT
- Total inputs are £2,000 plus £400 VAT.

He therefore makes profits of £28,000: £30,000 sales less £2,000 costs.

Now had Tom *not* been registered he could still have charged the public £18,000 as the total price they pay remains unchanged. This time, however, the total £18,000 excludes VAT and all ends up in Tom's pocket.

Dick will also only want to pay what he paid before which is £15,000 (remember he could recover the VAT paid so he really only paid £15,000).

By not being registered Tom will, of course, miss out on reclaiming the VAT on his purchases but we're only talking about a paltry £400.

In summary, without registering for VAT, Tom makes sales of £33,000 and has costs of £2,400 resulting in a profit of £30,600. That's £2,600 more than when he was VAT registered...not a bad return for a few back of the envelope calculations.

Looking back at the graph, Tom would be about half way along the bottom line and a little way up, falling squarely in the 'Don't register' part of the diagram.

Why Registering for VAT Can Be Beneficial

So much for businesses that have very little input VAT. If we move to the other end of the scale we will see that VAT registration can save you lots of money.

Harry, you may remember, bought furniture from Dick. Harry has just started a new business selling laptops and is VAT registered. His profit margins are very low – for every £1,000 of sales his cost price is £900.

Harry sells £30,000 worth of laptops during the year, made up as follows:

- £15,000 plus £3,000 VAT to VAT-registered customers.
- £15,000 plus £3,000 VAT to the general public.
- Total sales £30,000 plus £6,000 VAT.
- Total inputs £27,000 plus £5,400 VAT.

He therefore makes profits of £3,000: £30,000 sales less £27,000 costs.

He is making £100 profit per £1,000 of sales.

Now had Harry *not* been registered he could still have charged the public £18,000 because the price they pay remains unchanged. His VAT-registered customers would be unhappy about any increase so he would have to keep charging them £15,000.

Had Harry not registered he would therefore have made sales of £33,000 (£15,000 to the business customers plus £18,000 to private individuals). His costs would be £27,000 *plus VAT*, which he could not claim back, which comes to £32,400.

The final profit is therefore only £600, rather than £3,000 if he was VAT-registered.

If that wasn't bad enough, if you look at the sales to business customers, he is buying at £900 plus VAT (£1,080) and selling at £1,000. It doesn't take much business acumen to figure out that losing £80 per sale isn't a very good idea.

Looking back at the diagram above, Harry would be about half way along the bottom line and right up at the top, well inside the 'register' category.

From these examples we can see how being VAT-registered can either harm or benefit your business. We can also see that the VAT position can actually drive the type of business an organisation seeks.

If Harry wasn't VAT-registered he would have no incentive to sell to businesses at the prices given in the example and in practice would solve this issue by increasing his prices, which would presumably reduce demand.

VAT Registration Recap

Factors pointing towards early registration:

- High level of VAT registration amongst customers.
- High levels of input VAT (i.e. narrow margins).

Factors pointing toward delaying registration:

- Low levels of registration among customers.
- Low levels of input VAT.

In performing your own computations you should remember that you don't need a lot of accuracy to work out what to do, just a broad understanding of where you stand both now and where you are likely to be over the next 6 to 12 months.

If you perform computations along the lines of those in the above examples, rework the numbers several times, changing your assumptions. If the result comes out roughly the same each time then this should be good enough to make a decision.

If it is a close-run thing then it possibly doesn't matter much whether you're VAT registered or not. Generally speaking I would then err on the side of not registering as this will avoid the considerable extra administration effort required. You can see from the accounting part of this book that VAT makes bookkeeping somewhat harder.

Chapter 26

How to Register for VAT

Registering for VAT is a relatively straightforward process. The easiest way to do this is online, but it is still possible to apply with a paper form "VAT1".

Timing wise, in theory it should take between two and four weeks for your application to be processed. Speeds vary considerably and it can take eight or more weeks if there is a backlog. Extra security checks can be put in place for some sectors where there are historical issues of fraud such as in the import or export of small electrical items. The good news, however, is that online applications for small UK based service businesses often now arrive within 5 working days.

To start your online registration you can go here:

www.gov.uk/vat-registration/how-to-register

To obtain form VAT1 for a paper application, you can get this either from the National VAT helpline on 0300 200 3700 or here:

www.gov.uk/government/publications/vat-application-for-registration-vat1

General Tips

- I recommend you click the FAQs link on the registration page as they answer most of the common VAT registration queries.

- Use the online application form. This is somewhat easier to use than the paper version and it tends to get processed a lot quicker too.

- You can apply for all the VAT schemes at the same time as registering online, so do consider if any the schemes outlined in the following chapter can be used before you apply. This will save you time.

- The most awkward question on the online form asks about your business "SIC code" or Standard Industrial Classification code. There is a search tool within the online form which may help you find the code most relevant to your business, but it is rather basic. You may need to experiment with a range of keywords to find something appropriate.

- For those planning to register for the Flat Rate VAT Scheme, the SIC code you choose will determine the VAT rate you must use. However, you can go back and change the SIC code before submitting the application, so if you don't get the rate you expected, feel free to try something else!

- If you aren't sure how to answer a question on the form, check the website for help or ring the helpline – the staff are actually fairly well trained by helpline standards, although it can be worth calling twice to ensure they give you the same answer each time.

- If using the paper form make sure you provide a comprehensive answer to the 'Business activities' question (which asks you to outline your main and other business activities) – a one-line answer often results in further questions being asked.

- The bank account details can be added later if you are in the process of opening a business bank account.

- If your application is delayed, don't hesitate to chase it up with a call. Although HMRC claim otherwise, a significant proportion of clients with delayed registrations are active within 48 hours of a chaser call. If you don't hear from them call about a week before your intended registration date and then again on or just after the day on which you were supposed to be registered.

- Don't apply too far in advance. If you try and apply for a VAT number to commence more than 4 to 6 weeks in the future your application seems to get held back. From my experience advanced applications are more likely to be delayed and need chasing up, compared with applications made around 1 week before the commencement date.

Chapter 27

VAT Schemes - Saving You Time & Money

There are a number of special schemes available to help smaller businesses. Sometimes they can appear confusing but are worth investigating because they can make a big difference to your cash flow, accounting requirements and the amount you pay over.

The following section outlines the various schemes available, the benefits, the problems and who should consider which type of scheme. Please note the turnover levels stated below exclude VAT, in other words are quoted as the total invoice value before any VAT is added.

Annual Accounting Scheme

What is it?

- You pay nine VAT instalments, which are estimates of your VAT bill, and a balancing payment at the end of the year. The first instalment is paid three months after the start of the year.

Benefits:

- Only one VAT return to complete each year
- Helps with budgeting your cash flow

Eligibility:

- Turnover on joining the scheme must be under £1,350,000.
- You may remain in the scheme until your turnover reaches £1,600,000.

Suitable for:

- Stable businesses with predictable VAT levels.

- Businesses where the owner wants an accountant to complete the VAT return at the same time as the accounts – one annual return should lower your costs rather than having four completed during the year.

Unsuitable for:

- Erratic businesses. If your turnover drops you may be left having to pay more VAT than you actually received. You can revise your monthly payments, but this may mean leaving the scheme and a lot of extra admin. If turnover rises you may end up with quite a big VAT bill at the year-end.

- Businesses with significant levels of investment. You may have to wait up to 12 months to reclaim the cost of large capital investments.

Cash Accounting Scheme

What is it?

- You account for VAT only when payments are made or received, rather than when invoices are received or sent out (the normal 'accruals' basis).

Benefits:

- You don't pay out VAT until you are paid by your customers. Conversely, you can't reclaim VAT on invoices until you pay them.

- Accounting can be slightly easier if you use the cash basis rather than the accruals basis. In layman's terms this means you can complete your tax return using your bank statements to determine your income and expenses, instead of having to use invoices that have been issued or received.

Eligibility:

- Turnover under £1,350,000 on joining.

- You may remain in the scheme until your turnover reaches £1,600,000.

Suitable for:

- Most businesses that have to wait to be paid, for example those with business customers. This can make a serious difference to your cash flow.

- People using basic accounting techniques. Some basic accounting software only computes data for this scheme.

Unsuitable for:

- Businesses that receive payment soon after sale such as retailers.

- Businesses that pay their suppliers after they have been paid themselves. For example, if you get 90 days' credit on your purchases but get paid within seven days on your sales, this is likely to be unsuitable.

- Where you are likely to be receiving a VAT refund.

Flat Rate Scheme

What is it?

- Instead of computing your actual input VAT invoice by invoice, you ignore your expenses and calculate your VAT payment based on your turnover, using lower fixed rates

Benefits:

- Easy to compute your VAT liability

- Less emphasis on record keeping for VAT purposes

Eligibility:

- Turnover excluding VAT under £150,000

- Deregistration limit £230,000 including VAT. If HMRC are satisfied that the total value of your income in the next 12 months will not exceed £191,500, you may be eligible to remain in the scheme

Suitable for:

- Many businesses when the flat rate % is favourable

- When your input VAT is relatively low compared to others in your business sector

Unsuitable for:

- Many small service businesses (see below)

- Businesses with significant levels of exports that would not normally carry VAT

- Where the fixed rates are unfavourable to you

- If you have lots of investment spread over small invoices under £2,000 as this will not be eligible for reclaim

Calculating VAT under the Flat-Rate Scheme

Unlike the other schemes, which are all about cash flow and timing, this scheme actually changes the amount of VAT paid over to HMRC, so it is quite possible to end up paying over more or less VAT. You therefore need to consider this scheme carefully.

In Appendix 3 you will find a list of the rates available to different industry types. Your particular trade may not fit neatly into this list, but you should be able to get some idea of the rate you would have to use.

The rates are all lower than the current standard rate of 20% because you're not allowed to claim back VAT on your expenses. The quoted rates are applied to your turnover only. Whether or

157

not you're better off using this scheme depends on whether the lower VAT rate on your turnover adequately compensates you for being unable to recover VAT on your expenses.

The quoted rates are also deceptive. For example, '11%' in this context means 11% of the invoice value *including* VAT, not 11% of the net invoice as most people would imagine at first glance.

For a £1,000 + VAT invoice (£1,200 gross) the payment to HMRC will be £132 (11% of £1,200). You may have expected to only pay over £110 (11% of £1,000). So '11%' really means '12.9%' when compared directly with the normal rate of 20%.

You will see in Appendix 3 both the headline rates and the effective rates. The headline rates are those supplied by HMRC. The effective rates were computed by me and are directly comparable to the 20% rate that most people feel more comfortable using.

Whether or not the flat rate scheme is suitable to your business is essentially a maths question.

"Limited Cost Traders" from April 2017

If you run a small service business the flat rate scheme has limited use from April 2017.

In theory, the flat rates for each business category are neutral; that is to say the rates are equivalent to the net amount of VAT the average business in that category would pay over to HMRC under the regular VAT scheme. However, HMRC has been concerned that some businesses have significantly fewer expenses than is anticipated by their business category. As a result these businesses have been making quite sizable surpluses under the flat-rate scheme, reducing the VAT collected. HMRC calls these businesses "limited cost traders" and has introduced a new 16.5% rate with effect from 1 April 2017 to plug the VAT loss.

Because of the way VAT is calculated under the flat-rate scheme, the rate of 16.5% is equivalent to an effective VAT rate of 19.8%. For example, for a £1,000 + VAT invoice (£1,200 gross) the payment to HMRC is £198 (16.5% of £1,200). Thus businesses that have to use the 16.5% rate will pay pretty much the same VAT as most other VAT-registered businesses (20%) but will be unable to recover any VAT on their expenses.

A limited cost trader is defined as a business whose VAT inclusive spending on "relevant goods" during a VAT return period is either:

- Less than 2% of their VAT inclusive turnover
- More than 2% but less than £1,000 per year (£250 for a quarterly VAT return)

The test is carried out each time a VAT return is completed. Only spending on "relevant goods" is allowable.

"Relevant goods" *exclude*:

- Capital equipment (e.g. computers, phones, furniture)
- Vehicle costs including fuel
- Food and drink for the owners or staff
- Gifts, promotional items, donations
- Goods for resale or hiring out if this is not your **main** business activity (to prevent businesses starting a sideline selling goods to meet the test)

General services don't count, including professional fees, advertising, downloaded software or publications, stamps and rent payments.

Goods that do qualify must be incurred exclusively for your business. These may include:

- Goods purchased for resale in your main trade
- Stationery and other office supplies (e.g. printer cartridges)
- Gas and electricity used exclusively for your business (this means in practice a separate supply, not a home office)
- Standard software, provided on a disk
- Items consumed in your work

Most small service businesses simply won't have enough costs like these to meet the 2% threshold and may be tempted to buy relevant goods just to meet the test. To prevent this, goods bought solely to meet the test (e.g. goods that are stockpiled or given away) do not qualify, as they are not used exclusively for the purposes of your business.

If you are a retailer, café or other business that "buys and sells" then you will probably not fall under this category as the stock for a shop or food for a café's customers counts as "relevant goods".

Other Key Points about the Flat-Rate Scheme

- In the first year of VAT registration there is a bonus of 1% available. So if you would normally be on the 11% rate you actually only pay over 10% until the first anniversary of VAT registration. This bonus is often helpful where there are higher expenses for a new company.

- Any 'profit' made using the scheme is taxable. In other words, if you have charged £1,000 in VAT in the period, but the flat rate scheme allows you to only pay over £800, the extra £200 you are keeping hold of will become part of your taxable profits.

- You can reclaim VAT on large capital purchases (over £2,000) in the normal way.

- This scheme can be used in combination with the cash accounting scheme.

- The deregistration test (£230,000 of turnover including VAT) is performed on the anniversary of entry into the scheme. Therefore if you have a growing business you may not need to move back to the normal scheme right away.

- Buy-to-let rental income is normally exempt from VAT but is taxed at the flat-rate scheme percentage if it is earned by the same legal entity (individual) as the main business.

Do seek advice if you're considering using this scheme. You may need some help transferring between the normal scheme and the flat rate scheme. Moreover, I've had several clients who have used it for a few months and then transferred back as they didn't fully appreciate the rules and were losing money. This problem could have been avoided by seeking advice before making the switch.

More details of the VAT schemes can be found here under "Accounting for VAT": www.gov.uk/topic/business-tax/vat

Chapter 28

Clever VAT Registration Strategies

This section outlines some generic strategies that allow you to use the VAT system to your advantage.

Late Registration - Undercut the Competition

As we discussed before, where most of your customers are private individuals, registering for VAT is often not a good idea.

Take Roger, a legal executive who writes wills. None of his clients is VAT-registered and his input costs are negligible. Although Roger is good at what he does, he finds will writing is quite price sensitive. The local firm of solicitors charges £100 plus VAT, a total bill of £120. Roger considers four commercial choices:

- Register for VAT to appear larger than he is, charge £100+VAT (£120) and compete on service.

- Register for VAT and compete on price – say, charging £75+VAT for a total charge of £90.

- Don't register for VAT, but charge the same as the solicitors: £120.

- Don't register for VAT and compete on price, charging £90.

The following table shows the number of clients he estimates per month with each strategy:

Option	Price	No. Customers	Profit/Client	Total Profit
(1)	£100+VAT	10	£100	£1,000
(2)	£75+VAT	15	£75	£1,125
(3)	£120	10	£120	£1,200
(4)	£75	20	£75	£1,500

Clearly option (3) is the most profitable *per sale*. However, more money overall is being made with option (4) and Roger has to do twice as much work. As we can see VAT registration has made quite a difference to the business.

The main problem with this sort of approach is that the business model may get turned on its head if the business does really well and exceeds the VAT turnover threshold and is forced to register.

If this happened, Roger could either start to charge £75 plus VAT, which will lose him five customers, or perhaps consider selling at £62.50 plus VAT (a total price of £75), which will produce total profits of £1,250.

Either option looks quite unattractive when you consider how many more customers have to be handled. Roger may therefore choose to stay unregistered, sell at £120 so as not to spark a price war with the local solicitors and be happy to make £1,200 profit working part time.

In the real world if you attract customers by being cheap, you tend to lose them quite quickly when you put up your prices, so using this sort of strategy requires a lot of thought about where your business will be in the future. Staying 'niche' with a low turnover can often be a good alternative strategy.

Early Registration – Improve Your Cash Flow

Some businesses with high capital outlays, such as retail shops, will tend to have large expenses in the early months before much income has been earned. This is often financed through borrowing.

Although registration may not be compulsory for some months, reclaiming the VAT on the stock and fittings purchased could be extremely useful at a difficult time. It may therefore be worth opting for early registration to help the initial cash flow.

It is worth noting that the VAT on some start-up costs can often still be reclaimed when you eventually register, even if incurred up to three years earlier.

This applies to certain assets that are still in use but does not apply to stock that has already been sold by the time you register.

Selling Zero-Rated Supplies

If you are selling zero-rated supplies, for example if the majority of your customers are based outside the EU, then there really is little disadvantage to early registration. You can recover VAT on your expenses without having to change your selling prices as you won't need to add VAT to your sales prices.

Registering for Monthly Returns

If you are going to be claiming a VAT refund (for example, if you are making losses in the early days of trading or export much of your output) it may be worthwhile opting to complete a VAT return every month.

Although this may sound like a very bad idea from a paperwork point of view, receiving a monthly VAT refund from HMRC can be a real cash flow boost.

Temporary Registration

If you are running a business that is unlikely to breach the compulsory registration threshold you may find it beneficial to register for a short period of time, reclaim your input VAT on your start-up costs and then deregister.

There is some anti-avoidance legislation in this area, so this isn't something to 'try at home' – make sure you seek professional advice.

The main catch is that if you have assets on which you reclaimed more than £1,000 of VAT (i.e. total assets costing more than £6,000 including VAT) you will have to repay much of the VAT.

Example

Ted is a window cleaner. He starts up and buys a van, ladders and other equipment. His total costs are £5,000 plus VAT. Ted expects to receive around £15,000 a year in sales to householders. Generally speaking, registration would be a poor option – his input VAT other than his van is negligible (and he hopes to keep this for at least five years) and none of his clients are VAT registered.

By registering in the first three months, Ted is able to reclaim the VAT on his initial costs, which comes to £1,000. Unfortunately he does have to pay over VAT of £750 on his sales in his first quarter, but still comes out £250 ahead. This is equivalent to more than a week's work for Ted, and he is understandably quite pleased.

Due to the way the rules are written Ted could have registered within three years of buying the van and still reclaimed the VAT, provided it was still being used in the business. However, by registering at the beginning of trading Ted knows that his sales are probably somewhat lower than they will be in 12 months' time, and he gets his VAT back faster when cash is at its tightest.

The sting in the tail, however, is that on deregistering Ted could have had to pay back the VAT on the capital equipment if the amount involved is more than £1,000.

For example, if the van cost £10,000 the input VAT recovered in the first tax return would have to be paid back on deregistering, thereby making this a waste of time. There are further complications surrounding the value of the asset at the date of registration. As I mentioned before, this sort of planning isn't something to contemplate without proper advice but it can work for some businesses, especially where there is lots of cost upfront.

Section 8

How to Increase Cash Flow & Boost Your Profits

Chapter 29

Why is My Cash Flow Poor and How Do I Measure it?

"We have cash flow problems" is one of the most common complaints heard from small and medium sized businesses, especially when times are tough as they are at present.

However, I am firmly of the belief that every profitable business can have good cash flow *if* good cash flow practices are embedded in your business plan and *if* the cash is tightly managed on a day-to-day basis.

The main reasons cash flow problems occur are the following:

- Insufficient profits
- Lack of working capital
- Long cash cycle
- Poor collection procedures

Insufficient Profits

It may seem obvious but a lot of business claiming "cash flow" issues actually have far more fundamental profit issues. That is to say they simply do not have enough income to cover their overheads.

I am not going to directly address the point of profits in this section, other than to assume that we are always talking about profitable businesses.

That isn't to say loss-making business can't benefit from the techniques discussed but if you are making losses on a day-to-day basis your cash flow can only worsen in the medium to long term and the business will require external funding.

Lack of Working Capital

All businesses need some cash to carry out their day to day operations, taking into account seasonal swings and other variables specific to the business.

What I tend to find is that it is the irregular costs that catch people out. In particular, tax bills for VAT, corporation tax and income tax which tend to be the largest payments a small business will make during the year.

As we will see shortly you can reduce your working capital requirements by improving your "cash cycle" but fundamentally you should ensure the business has enough funds to cover:

- The basic day to day cash cycle
- VAT that you have collected on behalf of HMRC
- PAYE liabilities if you are an employer
- Corporation tax if you are a company
- Income tax if you are a sole trader/partnership or a higher rate tax payer with a company
- In an ideal world, a cash reserve to act as a buffer against hard times.

One major indicator of a business "at risk" of working capital issues is where the tax bills can only be paid by earning future profits, that is to say they have already been spent elsewhere.

Example

Let us meet Colin. Colin and his brother have a publishing company. For several years they have made £200,000 profit and paid corporation tax of around £40,000 per annum. The company draws up accounts to the end of December and the tax is not due until 1 October the following year. In the interim period the £40,000 owed in tax is invested in a new venture – which unfortunately fails and leaves them with nothing but debt.

During the current year the business struggles with advertising revenues down and some substantial bad debt. The business therefore only makes a small profit of £30,000. After payments to cover the directors much reduced living expenses there is simply no cash left in the business to pay the corporation tax bill, and an essentially profitable business with one bad year enters voluntary liquidation.

I should point out that this example is a real-life example from my client base. The owners took a risk with cash that in their opinion was just sitting in the bank, but in reality was not theirs to risk.

Had the company made its normal level of profit they would have been able to pay the tax bill out of that year's earnings but because profits where much reduced there was simply no cash left in the business. The banks would understandably not lend them the money and the directors were unable to inject any private capital having already suffered a very lean year. The only sensible option was to go into liquidation.

Length of Cash Flow Cycle

The cash flow cycle is a way of measuring the amount of time it takes to convert your goods or services into hard cash.

For a product based business this would typically be measured as:

The number of days it takes customers to pay from delivery

<u>Plus</u> the number of days stock you have on hand

<u>Less</u> the number of days you take to pay your suppliers for this stock

<u>Equals</u> the cash flow cycle

For a service business this would typically be measured as:

The number of days it takes customers to pay

<u>Plus</u> the average number of days between the service being provided and the invoice being issued

<u>Less</u> the number of days you take to pay your suppliers

<u>Equals</u> the cash flow cycle

Example

Going back to Colin's publishing company:

Customers took on average 60 days to pay.

Customers were billed at the end of the month in which their adverts appeared, and so on average 15 days after the publication date.

The main supplier invoiced at the end of the month which was an average of 15 days grace between printing and being invoiced.

Supplier invoices were paid promptly within 14 days.

60 + 15 = 75 days average credit offered, less 15 + 14 = 29 days on credit received = 46 days of credit that is required to be funded.

It's a good idea to think about your business cash cycle rather than concentrate only on the amount of time it takes customers to pay. This tool is a fairly blunt instrument and if your expenses are only a fraction of your sales five creditor days won't be the same amount of cash in the bank as five debtor days.

A long cash flow cycle is also a major barrier to growth. In the publishing example above, a new title required major investment because the publishing run is paid for on average 46 days BEFORE payment is received from the advertisers. In effect, the company had to fund the whole cost of publishing a new title from reserves, which is clearly a barrier to growth.

Poor Collection Procedures

This is normally where most guidance on cash flow management starts but, whilst very important on a day to day basis, your collection procedures should become a lot less important should you undertake the correct steps to minimising your cash flow cycle.

We will now take a detailed look at how to do just that.

Chapter 30

Smart Business Strategies for Strong Cash Flow

You can actively manage the general risk of hitting cash flow problems by managing three key aspects of your business strategy

- Undue influence of big customers
- The flexibility of your cost base
- Exposure to debts

Undue Influence of Big Customers

The first step is to consider your customer base and risk.

Many smaller businesses are heavily reliant on a few key contracts, which can cause cash flow problems, especially when the customers use their power to force unfavourable terms on you.

Example

Back to Colin from the previous chapter. Out of the normal £1 million turnover, a key advertiser provides £300,000 worth of advertising per annum, 30% of the total. They normally pay on 60 days, and so typically have £50,000 outstanding.

The advertiser is struggling and decides arbitrarily to pay after 120 days, making the average amount outstanding £100,000.

Colin's firm simply doesn't have another £50,000 to fund its working capital. Colin has a stark choice – stop placing the adverts (which would make a huge difference to the profitability of the title), swallow the terms, or haggle like mad.

This is a horrible position to be in but a very common one when a business has a few key customers who can exert their power.

Had this been a £3,000 per year customer the decision would have been simple: stop printing and pursue the debt.

So what can be learned from this example? You should think about your key customers and how much credit you can extend to them. If you are over reliant on a key customer you should think about trying to reduce their influence over your business so that you can at any time stand up and say "no" if you need to.

The supermarkets are past masters at this tactic. They tend to be by far the largest and sometimes only customer of their suppliers. This dominant position is then used to squeeze their suppliers dry and insist on all manner of harsh terms.

Keeping it Flexible

If your cost base is largely fixed (for example your premises costs, wage bill and supply costs), then changing your overheads to match variations in your sales is very difficult.

If, on the other hand, your business has flexible overheads because you have a short-term office lease, employ a mixture of flexible staff and subcontractors, and can turn on or off your supplies, you are in a strong position to react to change.

Going back to the assertion that "cash flow" problems are often just profit problems, a business with large overheads that suffers a reduction in trade will tend to hit cash flow problems very quickly as the outgoings stay the same while the income plummets.

The conundrum is that, generally speaking, entering long term contracts for the lease of premises, the employment of staff and securing supplies will generally generate much bigger profits, not to mention delivering a higher quality product or service too.

The balancing act for most businesses is taking the additional profit when it all goes well but having the flexibility to vary overheads rapidly when conditions deteriorate.

Only the individual business owner can make the right decision for their own business, but these sorts of issue can be critical to long term success so are well worth considering formally.

Make sure you have contingency plans in place. What if we lose a major contract? What if we gain everything we have quoted for? Having these in place helps you stay one step ahead and take decisive steps when they count. Often businesses fail due to management not reducing their overheads quickly enough when they had a chance to do so.

Managing Your Exposure to Debt

Managing your exposure to bad debt is often a difficult balance. The fewer the customers, the bigger the potential problem.

In blunt terms, the longer someone owes you money for, the more chance they will go bust before they pay you back.

The bigger that customer is the bigger the risk you are taking.

If you normally extend, say, three months credit to a key customer you are in effect risking three months of sales.

The problem tends to lie with being strict with customers – businesses have a natural tendency to want to support their major customers in order to strengthen relationships – which can often mean extending extra credit right the risk of never being paid is greatest.

Tip. One thing you can do is bury in your contracts with smaller incorporated customers a clause of director's personal guarantee. This ensures you still have some comeback in the event of business failure. The banks do this routinely – check the terms and conditions on your overdraft!

If you don't have such a clause and you suspect a business is in difficulty then you could agree to continue to supply that business, but **only** on the condition that the transaction is underwritten by the directors personally. If the directors won't sign then your worries were probably well founded and it is better to make a tactical withdrawal than throw further money their way. You have at least given them a chance.

Chapter 31

Great Billing Tactics to Get the Cash Rolling In

In this chapter we look at not just how many days credit to offer customers, but more fundamentally how to think about your business and how to reduce your cash flow cycle. It is quite possible to have a low risk business that collects payments well before goods or services are paid for. It does however take quite a lot of thinking about.

Should I Offer Credit At All?

It's your business and therefore very much your choice if you offer credit. Many businesses structure themselves so that no credit is actually offered; all payments are in advance or on delivery, although in many areas this would make life very hard commercially.

What works for your business is going to depend very much on what you do, but it is worth thinking about why different businesses have different structures, and how these can be applied to your own enterprise, even where it might not be the 'normal' thing to do.

Payments in advance, including deposits, are typically requested where:

- A service has to be performed at a particular time and the time slot cannot be re-sold, such as holiday accommodation.

- Something has to be made to order, placing risk on the supplier that the goods cannot be sold to someone else (a bespoke suit, for example).

- There is no effective mechanism to receive payment on receipt. For example, with mail order goods it would horrendous trying to get payments at the door step!

- There is an annual licence, such as for software.

Payment at the time of delivery tends to occur where:

- There are a large number of small transactions, such as in general retail.

- There is significant risk of non-payment, such as in a crowded pub.

- Transactions are with the general public.

Payments by invoice in arrears tend to occur where:

- The price is variable and cannot be calculated until after the event has occurred.

- The outcome of the activity is variable and the customer may not be willing to pay until they are satisfied with the result.

- It's a business to business transaction.

Example

I recently advised an executive private car hire company, heavily reliant on a small number of contracts from big businesses ferrying senior member of staff between meetings and airports. Let's call it Joe's Cabs. The original owner ended up in bankruptcy partly due to excessive overheads, partly due to bad cash flow. At the core of the rescued business was however a perfectly decent and profitable activity.

The original plan was simple – the self employed drivers drove all month, they billed Joe for their time, and a single invoice was sent by Joe's Cabs to each of a handful of commercial customers.

The sales invoices should have been paid in 14 days, just in time to pay the drivers.

In the event the end customers paid closer to 90 days than 14, and often there where disputes about which trips had or hadn't occurred. This left Joe's Cabs with a number of angry drivers he couldn't afford to pay.

The rescue plan was equally simple. The journeys were already booked using a sophisticated online system that had an optional payment module. All it needed was turning on!

The cost to Joe's Cabs was a 2% credit card transaction fee, but as the drivers where now being paid weekly the new owner was able to recoup some of this from the drivers in return for quick payment.

The end customers were apparently not the slightest bit concerned how the billing was settled, and we had turned a nightmare cash flow situation into a far less risky business.

Sanctions to Force Payment

In the above example the business was changed so that the activity was not undertaken until payment had been received. If you are able to delay perform your service until full payment has been made you are very much in the driving seat.

In my own business a client doesn't have their tax return filed until they have paid. It's a very simple and effective control.

Perhaps you are a wedding photographer supplying your pictures on CD. If so I will hazard a guess that if you supply in the first instance proofs with your copyright across the front you will get paid a lot sooner than simply enclosing your invoice with the final usable copies of your work.

It's all fairly basic stuff but it can have a huge impact on your cash flow.

You may be thinking "but I can't do that, it's not the done thing". Well it might not be for anyone else but it's your business so it's up to you to make the rules.

Be creative. There is often some way in which you can have a subtle hold over a client to ensure you get full payment without being too intrusive.

Timing Your Invoices

Not every business is able collect money in advance of the service being offered but many can certainly improve their cash flow dramatically by bringing forward the date when an invoice is sent out.

Example

Do you recall Colin and his brother who own the publishing business?

His customers paid after around 60 days on invoices issued 15 days after the publishing date. Colin paid their main suppliers on average 29 days after publication, making a cash flow cycle of 46 days.

To my mind there are two easy wins here:

1. *Issue the invoices on the day the magazine is published. This would have saved 15 days on average. Many businesses only seem to bill at the end of the month which, in my opinion, is just plain daft.*

2. *Better still, issue the invoice when the space is **ordered,** which was typically at least 15 days prior to publication, saving 30 days.*

With step 2, this should bring the payment date to around 45 days after publication on average. With the printers being paid around 29 days after publication, the total cash flow cycle would fall from 46 days to around 15. In other words, this simple step would have reduced the working capital requirements of the business by 2/3rds.

The customers would probably not really have noticed either if the change was phased in over several editions.

Moreover with a bit of work the 60 day payment terms could probably be whittled down to 45, reducing the working capital requirement to nil, with the average payment occurring one month after the publication date.

Finally, with shorter terms it would have been a lot easier to threaten customers with being taken out of the next publication for non-payment, rather than allowing them to be listed three or four times before serious action is taken. You only have to drop someone's advertising once to get them used to the idea that payment is not optional.

Going back to sanctions, had this been my business I would simply have not run the advert unless payment had been received in full by the publication date. I had this conversation regularly with Colin who was adamant this was not possible. Admittedly this is quite an aggressive stance and Colin is a very nice chap, but 'nice chaps' don't always make it in business, and this one has a bankruptcy behind him and I imagine won't be quite so accommodating in his new venture.

Some key areas where businesses really do not help themselves:

- Billing at the end of the month rather than on the supply of the goods/services.

- Billing in arrears when invoices could easily be issued in advance. This is particularly common for service based industries, such as regular support services, when it's quite common to pay at the start of the contract.

- Not sending an invoice at all as they are forgotten about.

I will leave this topic with another real life horror story of bad billing procedures.

Example

John is a plumber (my plumber actually) and likes bending pipes but he isn't much interested in money, well apart from when he hasn't got any. Despite charging a not inconsiderable daily rate and being in high demand he has been bankrupt more than once.

The reason for this became quite apparent last year.

John made a lovely job of my bathroom but six months later, and despite my ringing him to ask for it, I still didn't have the invoice.

I needed a minor bit of work doing and although John remembered he had not sent a bill for the bathroom, he flatly refused a cheque payment for his original work, or that day's work, saying he would send me a bill next week once he had worked out the costs of all the parts. The bill didn't arrive.

On the third visit to service the boiler some time later, and nearly a year after the original work, John still refused payment, and in the end I wrote out a cheque of what I thought I owed and tucked it into his top pocket as he left. I really don't like to owe people money!

Now this is a pretty extreme example and had it not happened to me I wouldn't have believed someone could be so sloppy with their billing. John must simply not bill thousands of pounds worth of work annually. This example shows that forgetting the basics can have a catastrophic effect on a small business.

John and I had a long talk incidentally and he agreed that all he needed to do once a job was finished was write up a receipt in his van, present this to the householder whilst putting his tools away and not leave until he had been paid. Whether John has taken this suggestion up we will see. I do hope so. He is a good plumber but hasn't got much of a business brain.

Don't be a John with your paperwork! Build your billing into your every day routine, and not only will it be out of the way, you will almost certainly get paid more quickly and the right amount. Any disputes can also be sorted out on the spot while it's all fresh in everyone's mind.

Agreeing Terms

Talking of disputes, one key thing to mention is that if you are working for someone; make sure you agree on the terms.

For product based businesses, price tends to be key and clearly stated and agreed upfront.

For services businesses things are often a lot more vague, but that very vagueness can lead to the possibility of disputes about the final bill, which in turn means slower payments and bad feelings on both sides.

Some basic techniques you can use are as follows:

- **In writing**. Ensure all jobs are quoted for in writing, clearly stating what's included and anything that's specifically excluded. An email is helpful, especially to ask your customer to confirm they are happy with the quote.

- **Clear estimates**. If billing hourly, give a clear estimate of how many hours are likely to be involved and the total bill.

- **Changes.** Where estimates are too low, inform the customer early on that the final bill is likely to be more than estimated and explain why. We all dread that call when the car is in the garage telling you that your service is going to cost a lot more, but it's better to find out before the work starts than when you turn up to pay.

- **Fixed fees.** If you undertake the same job regularly, offer a tariff of fixed fees. Research has shown that people will actually prefer to pay a higher fixed fee that is certain than a variable fee which comes out on average less. From my own business I find that fixed fees make for happier clients, and it's a lot easier to bill too!

- **Sign off.** Once the job is complete see if you can get the customer to express in some way that they are happy with it. As we will see later, this acceptance can be important later on if your bill is later disputed. A "sign off" can be incorporated in anything from a formal consultant's report, where the client agrees to the recommendations, to a simple follow-up email asking if the customer is happy.

Invoicing Long-term Projects

If you are involved in long-term projects taking several months you should ensure you take stage payments to match your outgoings. Typically a good contract will outline:

- A deposit on sign up
- Key interim targets against which an invoice can be raised
- Final sign off
- Adjuster clauses for changes to the scope of the project

The point of doing this is to reduce the risk on both sides – the customer is unlikely to want to pay upfront several months before a project is complete, the supplier should be unwilling to work for free for long periods, especially if substantial costs are incurred.

Example

Richard is fed up designing websites for people who don't pay for them.

He therefore asks for a 25% deposit upfront before work commences. This ensures the end client has something to lose if the work is cancelled before it has reached the next stage.

Once the site layout is ready, the key features are in place and the customer approves the site in principle, he invoices the next 50%.

On receipt of the payment (75% now paid) the final testing and polishing phase commences and the finished site is made available to the client. The final tranche of 25% is then due for payment.

Richard has lowered his risk of default substantially, but at the same time the customer has a pretty good idea of what they are going to get and shouldn't object to the interim payments.

Identity Checks & Credit Checks

If you are going to offer credit to someone, it doesn't half help if you know exactly who they are and if they can afford to pay you. This is very obvious when you write it out, but not so obvious it would seem in the real world of business.

For online retailers the principles are generally fairly well ingrained and unless the delivery address ties up with the credit card details you don't send the goods out.

For general service businesses it is not uncommon to essentially offer informal credit to customers without knowing much about them.

The traditional route here is formal credit checking. On the one hand it can provide valuable information about a customer and their credit worthiness, highlighting danger situations such as individuals or businesses with a string of county court judgements against their names.

On the other hand, the information is often out of date given it could be based on historical accounts up to two years old. Moreover credit checking is often merely a "tick box" exercise of little practical value based on some arbitrary rules. Crucially credit checking a business at the start of your business relationship won't help pick up changes over time.

For your own business you really have to just apply a big dollop of common sense. In the first instance you need to know who your customer is, so unless it's obvious, check their full name and address with some ID before offering credit. A simple letter that requires a response (for example your contract) sent to the customer's stated home address can ensure you know where they live.

Moreover the bigger the credit line, the more thorough you need to be. If you deal with a small number of large businesses and need to extend credit then it really is necessary to carry out some due diligence on their credit worthiness. That massive order out of the blue should be treated with a little scepticism before you get too carried away with the celebrations.

My personal approach is actually not to credit check but to only offer small orders on a tight reign to new customers. I often take a deposit or full payment in advance if I have any doubts.

What Credit Terms Should I Offer?

Assuming you have no option but to offer credit to your customer, the next thing to decide is for how long?

The most common credit term offered in the UK is 30 days. However the key question I have for you is, "why?" I often have a conversation with my clients about this topic, and it invariably goes something like this:

> Me   *"Can I ask why you offer 30 days credit terms?"*
> Client *"erm….."*
> Me   *"Seriously, why did you settle on 30 days?"*

> Client "(big pause) well everyone else does, its standard in my industry"
>
> Me "What would you say was standard for accountants?"
>
> Client "erm......30 days?"
>
> Me "I would say that is about right. Do you know what terms are on our agreement?"
>
> Client "erm, I can't remember us discussing that"
>
> Me "Exactly my point!"

I don't tend to go in for torturing my clients just for fun, it's a serious point about out how credit terms are set. In my day to day business I am almost always asked about what the fee will be but very rarely about when it is due for payment.

Have a think about the last time a customer asked you about credit terms before signing your contract. Seriously! Have a think.

It doesn't happen much does it? Often they are no more than an afterthought. If this applies to you, why are you giving away something for nothing?

My rule of thumb for payments is that you can take your terms and double them and that is how long it will take you to get paid.

It might help thinking about why this works from the other side of the fence. If you receive an invoice and the payment terms are, say, 7 to 14 days, the normal reaction is to pay it or, at least, put it in the pile for payment this week or at the month end.

If you receive an invoice with longer terms, I don't know about you but I am very unlikely to pay it right away. However, if it floats around my desk for a month or so there is a fair chance the cleaner will move it or it will mysteriously end up in the shredder or be accidently filed in the wrong place. The next time I will think about it is when a reminder is sent out in a month's time, by which time I may well have even forgotten what it was for.

Coming back round to the point of view of the business sending out invoices, you can gently chase a 7 day term invoice after a week while its fresh, push it a little harder after two weeks and get quite firm after a month, but with a 30 day invoice there is not a lot you can do for a month, and you can't really be firm until a good two months have elapsed.

Changing Terms for Existing Clients

That's all very well for new clients I hear you say, but how about existing ones?

Well it depends how cheeky you want to be but assuming you can implement new terms and conditions, then just slip in the change next time around and move towards the terms you want and see what happens.

If coming down from 30 days to 7, I would probably try 14 for a couple of months before switching to 7. In particular, where you are dealing with larger businesses which have their own accounts departments, the change often won't be noticed. In the worst case scenario you can say you (cough!) made a simple paperwork error and will issue future invoices with the original terms.

I must admit I was rather sceptical about this idea the first time it was suggested to me, not least because I was at the time in the firing line for all the complaints, but having implemented it for some quite large businesses across literally hundreds of customers without so much as a single question being raised, I have no hesitation in suggesting this strategy to you, for no other reason than it works!

Putting the Right Information on Your Invoices

This is an easy win for most businesses that issue invoices. Does your invoice clearly and fully state the following?

- Who it should go to (it may be the accounts department, or it may be the person you deal with)

- The due date for payment

- Exactly what is being charged for

- How to pay, that is to say full bank details, who the cheque should be made out to and the address to send it to

- Your contact name and phone number for queries

- If it is not obvious, the person who made the order and the customer's own purchase order (PO) reference if required. This is often helpful with larger companies where the accounts department will ask for the budget holder to "sign off" your invoice before payment is released.

If you don't include all the relevant details then it shouldn't be terribly surprising when cheques arrive in the wrong name or if lots of people simply do not bother to pay. I would say on average *a third* of invoices I see on a day to day basis from small businesses simply fail to provide full payment instructions, which means its hard work for their customers to actually pay them.

Payment Methods

The payment methods you offer can have a small but important influence on the speed funds arrive in your account.

Cash is clearly the quickest but outside of retail cash is not a popular option. The others in order of speed are:

- **BACS transfer** (also known as a bank transfer). Since the banking world got its act together recently, payments often arrive in your bank account on the same day as payment. You do of course need to encourage this by clearly stating your details on your invoices.

- **Credit card**. This can in some instances mean a long wait for payment, but where you have credit card facilities set up directly with your bank, you will normally get paid within two or three days of the card being processed.

- **Cheque**. The humble cheque is probably the slowest method of payment. Two to three days to arrive in the post, possibly a day or two for you to find the time to go to the bank and another 3 or 4 working days to clear. Total time is likely to be at least one working week and often closer to two.

Having worked long and hard getting your invoices out as early as possible, it makes good business sense to also ensure your method of payment is as efficient as possible.

Tip: For recurring monthly payments, most online payment processors offer a recurring transaction option for credit cards which can be a useful alternative to Direct Debits, which tend not to be accessible to smaller businesses.

Chapter Recap

Throughout this chapter we have looked in some detail at the timing of payments, trying to ensure you get paid ideally before you provide your goods or services and, if not, arranging your business so that you have a hold over your customer to make it in their interests to pay.

Where an invoice is issued after the event we have looked at why it is important to know who your customer is, get those invoices issued promptly and accurately with sufficient information to get them paid, and not give away credit needlessly.

Many of these steps are quite small when taken on their own but together they really can make the difference between the success and failure of your business.

In the next chapter we look at the art of collecting those invoices.

Chapter 32

Effective Credit Control

In order to have effective credit control, the first thing you need is effective information about:

- What sales invoices have been issued
- What sales invoices have been paid

That might sound rather obvious but I am constantly surprised how many businesses simply do not know what invoices are outstanding and consequently don't chase them in a timely manner. All the focus is on sales and production and very little on getting the cash in.

Using the techniques we have discussed elsewhere in this book about keeping records you should be able to:

- Keep an up-to-date list of your sales invoices
- Mark them off when paid

If you are paid by cheque it is quite simple to mark your sales as paid as they come past your desk. If you receive most of your payments via bank transfer then it's probably a very good idea to use online banking so that you can view your account live rather than once a month when the bank statement arrives. Many transfers are now occurring same day rather than within three working days, as was the previous norm.

The key to this is simply discipline. The discipline to check, and for most businesses that means daily, the movement on your bank account, what transactions need to be processed in your accounts, and who may need a prod to get a payment coming your way. Once a month really isn't enough for most businesses.

Once you know what money is outstanding you can move on to the collection procedure.

As an aside, do make sure someone hasn't already paid. There really is nothing more embarrassing (and I speak from regrettable experience!) than giving a customer a hard time for not paying a bill that they have already paid.

Collection Procedures

The best collection procedures are pre-defined but flexible enough to allow for individual circumstances.

The point of having a pre-defined procedure is that you don't have to make a decision about what steps to take, you just keep on following the procedure until you get paid. This is especially important for those of us who hate chasing for money as you tend to put it off. A good procedure can also be delegated if you have administrative assistance.

Typical procedures are outlined in the following table. Obviously what works for you will depend on the relationship you have with your customers, the level of regular contact and the volume of invoices generated. Time scales may well be a lot longer or shorter than listed here.

Timing	Action	Reason
Just before the date of payment	Polite email confirming the customer is happy with the service and confirming they have received the paperwork.	Polite prompt. Ensure the customer has everything they need to pay and there are no disputes.
Just after date of payment	Polite email noting that no payment received by due date. Enclose copy of invoice.	Enforces the message that due dates should be adhered to. Make sure they have the paperwork.
1-2 weeks after due date	Firmer reminder email. Directly ask when you should expect payment.	Keep yourself up the priority list. Try and get the customer to make a promise to pay which confirms your invoice as valid.
2-3 weeks after due date	Call your customer to discuss their overdue account. You may need to do this several times if they are being elusive!	Listen to problems they may genuinely have. Make the issue of payment a serious one.
One month over due	Formal letter outlining the consequences of failing to pay, For example putting the account on hold and ultimately leading to a CCJ. Enclose the invoice again.	Make it quite clear that the invoice needs to be paid and you are serious. Putting the account on hold reduces your exposure and puts the customer under pressure.
4-6 weeks overdue	Keep calling. You may now be at the leaving message stage. If so leave lots, landline, mobile, email everything you can.	Keep up the pressure if ignored. Try and make it easier for them to pay. You may be able to force a payment plan at this point.
6-8 weeks overdue	Issue a formal "letter before action". Send via registered post. Call and explain politely why you have done this. Stop calling (yes really!).	This is a 'frightener' aimed at very reluctant payers. The point of not calling is to get them to call you and signal game over - this is very serious.
2 months overdue or on default of payment plan	Commence formal collection procedures via a CCJ.	A last resort.

Now for most regular repeat business clients you shouldn't ever have to get beyond a couple of calls and a stiff letter.

The best way to do it is to be brisk and business like and at the start try and build it around something else if you can, such as feedback about what you have done for them, or the next bit of work.

I certainly wouldn't give them a sob story about why you need the money to buy food to feed your children, simply state that the invoice is overdue and those are the terms. In the vast majority of occasions I find that the customer is actually rather apologetic and accepts that they are in the wrong for not having paid.

The deeper into the process you go the more entrenched it tends to get and you have to really make a decision about whether you want this customer or not. The less you care about keeping them, the harder you can push it on the basis that they won't ever be coming back.

Understanding Your Customers Payment Systems

If you have a few larger customers it often pays to work out the payment triggers on the other side to ensure the time you spend chasing invoices is effective.

Often a procedure in a larger business will be as follows:

- Functional manager (probably your contact) signs your invoice as goods/services received.
- Invoice passed to the budget holder for approval.
- Invoice then passed to accounts.
- Once sufficient triggers are passed, this is passed for payment.
- Payment authorised by the company accountant and made.

Your invoice may be stuck at any one of these points – your aim is to find out where it sticks and kick it through to the next level. The accounts staff will invariably blame the budget holder. The budget holder will invariably blame the accounts department. Such is life!

Once an invoice has been approved, the accounts department may well sit on it until certain trigger points occur. These could be:

- Your invoice is sufficiently overdue (e.g. 15, 30, 60, or even 90 days old).
- You have chased the invoice up. Many companies don't pay unless you ask. Period.
- You have chased up enough times. Sometimes payment will only rather meanly occur on, for example, the third call.

All this is rather exasperating but this is how real businesses operate in order to conserve their own cash flow. If you can work out what the triggers are than more often than not you can work out what to do to get paid quickly. It may just be a case of emailing your contact, ensuring the invoice has been passed to accounts, and then calling accounts a few days later to check what payment run it will be included on.

Won't Pay, Can't pay, or Dispute

It is always worth bearing in mind that there may be several reasons why an invoice has not been paid.

- The invoice is in dispute. Rightly or wrongly.
- The customer physically can't pay you as they don't have the money to do so – a "can't pay"
- They have chosen not to pay – a "won't pay"

Dispute. For invoices in dispute, the key is to get agreement. You may often find that "won't pays" will dispute an invoice part of the way through the process. It is therefore essential that you get an early promise to pay, preferably non-verbal such as by email. Once you have that agreement it is very hard for them to wriggle out of it, and threats of a CCJ become more credible.

If there is a genuine dispute then you clearly need to sort it out as soon as possible. Given most disputes only tend to get worse over time, as memories get foggier and positions become more entrenched, it is very important to identify disputed invoices early on. Going back to the credit control procedure, one of the first steps is to check your customer is happy.

"Can't Pays". These are often the hardest to crack despite the customer normally being responsive. On the one hand you need to ensure you are high up the priority list of payments (invariably *some* invoices are being paid, just not yours), on the other hand it can be helpful in the longer term to be accommodating if you want to do business again. It is often very hard to establish genuine cases of "can't pay", all you can do is keep talking to the customer and it's up to you to decide if you believe them or not. Often a payment plan is suitable for such situations to get your invoice gradually paid off but this won't help if they are heading for bankruptcy anyway.

"Won't Pays". Perversely these are often the easiest to deal with – you just keep on at them and grind them down, but they often masquerade as "disputes" or "can't pays'". Generally the best way to deal with "won't pay's" is to rattle along quickly towards a CCJ when your 'letter before action' will often be the main trigger for payment.

Putting Clients on "Stop"

One of the hardest things to do with a reluctant debtor is to force payment when you have no hold over the business. When you do have a hold you may be surprised how quickly they can pay when they really want to.

Where there is an ongoing relationship you can put a client "on stop" which means putting their account on hold and no longer providing further goods or services. How big a threat this is will depend entirely on how your customer views your business relationship. If the customer can easily switch suppliers then this won't work. But if it takes time to secure supplies then this can be a winning strategy.

The main problem with this approach is that your sales brain won't want to put a large customer on stop, but your accounting brain will tell you there is no point working for someone if you are not getting paid. This conflict can make people reluctant to do it but it is a very effective tool, especially when you are dealing with larger businesses where your contact person doesn't necessarily realise (or care) that the finance department is not paying you. The second you stop supplying it will be a different story.

I have tried this tactic several times, this is one example:

Example

A businesses supplies a manufactured product and associated spares. During a quiet time, with only spares being ordered, the problem customer (which accounts for over 20% of the supplier's annual sales) was placed on stop.

This caused significant disruption to the customer's business. Various senior figures from the customer called their counterparts at the supplier. All of them are rather apologetic. The customer's shell-shocked accountant received a dressing down from senior members of the customer's staff. The end result was full payment of a substantial sum within two weeks including previously disputed invoices stretching back two years.

From that point on the supplier has enjoyed red carpet treatment from the customer's accounts department.

Extreme, but it really does work. Fortunately I was the supplier's accountant and not the customer's! For smaller businesses the impact can be equally startling. It really does show you are serious about getting paid and often won't actually damage your relationship with the customer, especially if that relationship is separate to the payment function.

Payment Plans

Payment plans are sometimes agreed with customers to break down big overdue invoices into smaller stage payments. This can be something as simple as a one page document signed by both parties with the agreed terms laid out.

The key advantages are:

1. Admission of liability which helps with a CCJ
2. Ability to build in extra costs such as statutory interest and costs of collection
3. They do sometimes work

For my money (1) and (2) are far more important than (3).

Often payment plans end up simply being a delaying tactic. For this reason I would not normally enter into one without:

1. The first payment being made immediately
2. The payments being weekly over a maximum of 6-8 weeks
3. Any default resulting in the full sum becoming due

My favourite tactic with such plans is to insist on the reluctant debtor committing to the plan by writing out a post dated cheque for each and every due payment. Now whilst the customer could of course easily cancel these cheques I have found it doesn't happen very often, not least of course because it would cost them £10 or more per cheque, and so long as there are sufficient funds available in the account I have found such payments clear.

Debt Collection Agencies and Solicitors

There are lots of debt collection agencies around who will chase your debts for you. These agencies are most suitable when you want no further contact with the customer and when you don't think the debtor is taking your collection efforts very seriously.

Merely placing a debt with an agency is often enough to make a debtor sit up and take notice. This is despite the fact that most agencies generally will not do anything different to you – they tend to just pester with calls and letters. It is very rare to see a debt collection agency dispatch heavy set gentlemen who crack their knuckles in reception!

Solicitors are often used for larger amounts and to help collect the debts more formally through the courts. In particular a "letter before action" from a solicitor can have a much greater impact than one on your own headed paper. Fees for these tend to be very low, often only £10 or £20 as they are often done on a 'loss leader' basis.

Generally you should look for a solicitor with a specialist debt recovery department who undertakes this sort of work on a daily basis. Such solicitors can give very valuable advice on using the county courts.

DIY County Court Judgments

If it comes to it you can actually pursue a debtor yourself through the county courts using the "money claim online" system. I would only suggest doing this after you have used a solicitor for your first few so you understand the process.

All you do is fill out the form, make your claim and the debtor will receive a summons. The response is normally in writing – it is actually quite unusual for either side to end up in a court room. The "court" is merely a clerk processing the paperwork.

For more information: www.gov.uk/make-money-claim-online

A CCJ should mark the end of the road. It is very unlikely a client forced to pay in such a manner will ever come back. Also be careful of throwing "good money after bad". It is pointless obtaining a CCJ against a customer who has already got an armful of them. If they are unwilling or unable to pay, enforcement could be a costly and futile exercise.

Hurrah They Paid – Now What?

After a lengthy haggle to get paid many businesses then face a bit of a dilemma. Sometimes it's obvious that the customer should be shown the door. At other times you may find that you are quite happy to deal with them again, provided they pay their invoices on time.

In my own business my approach is to simply write to the customer, thank them for their payment, and enclose their new terms and conditions. These will invariably include the requirement to pay upfront in the future.

If the customer agrees to the terms, then it's problem solved. If they don't come back, then that's generally fine too, unless you are overly reliant on the customer.

This comes back full circle to the structural issues we discussed at the beginning of this part of the guide. If you simply can't say "no" to a customer and they realise this, then your customer has all the power and may choose to use it.

General Collection Tips

I will leave this section with a few additional general tips:

- **Notes!** Make lots of notes showing dates, times of calls, promises made and disputes raised. I normally pop a list of these into a formal letter which tends to hammer home the point rather unsubtly of broken promises and the amount of effort you have taken to collect the debt.

- **Follow up**. If a customer has promised to pay and the payment doesn't arrive, follow it up right away. If you wait two weeks until you next have your credit control hat on, any pressure built up will have been lost. Remember electronic payments may now hit your account same day, so if your customer has promised to pay, check!

- **Dealing with false promises**. If a customer claims to have paid that day online or will be "putting a cheque in the post", don't be afraid to politely ask if they would mind showing you a screen shot of the payment coming out of their account or scanning and emailing a copy of the cheque. This can force them to actually make the payment that would otherwise have been left another week or two.

- **Don't put it off.** If your plan is to chase payments every Tuesday, make sure you do it. You always feel better after making the call. I have been chasing debts for years now in all sorts of different roles, and it still makes me slightly nervous to pick up the phone and ask where my money is! I tend to put a reminder in my diary system to nag me.

- **Good Cop/Bad Cop**. If there are several of you involved in the business, you can play a game of "Good Cop, Bad Cop". "Good Cop" is the regular contact who handles the normal polite chasing up of invoices. "Bad Cop" is wheeled in to do the hard chasing, which can help preserve the business relationship as well as to signal an end to slow payment.

- **Chasing is Stressful**. Don't take it too personally. Some people get very worked up when debtors don't pay. Most business get *some* bad debt now and again.

Section 9

Other Issues for the Small Business

This section deals with some additional issues that affect many small businesses. In Chapter 33 we look at using Accounting Software as opposed to spreadsheets. In Chapter 34 I review the practical aspects of taking on your first employee and how to deal with the taxman. In Chapter 35 I look at how to get help with your accounting by employing a bookkeeper or accountant.

Chapter 33

The Best Accounting Software

So far this book has focused mainly on using basic spreadsheets to do all your bookkeeping. Given that your objective should be to obtain the most information with the least effort, there's a lot to be said for doing it this way.

As your business grows, however, you may find that spreadsheets aren't powerful enough, unless the volume of transactions is quite small or you are quite diligent with your record keeping.

This is where using business software comes into the picture.

The main advantages of using software over spreadsheets are as follows:

- **Accuracy.** You are less likely to accidentally overwrite or delete data, and you remove the inherent risk of errors in formulas in your spreadsheets.

- **Management information.** Even the basic reports produced by accounting packages tend to be a lot better than you can produce easily using a spreadsheet.

- **Instant VAT returns.** Most software packages can produce automated VAT returns once sales and expense information has been entered.

- **Speed.** Bank reconciliations and other accounting controls are generally quicker.

- **Stock management.** 'Real time' stock information is available if you use business software.

- **Cost savings.** You may save money when your accountant completes your tax return as he may receive better quality information from proper bookkeeping software than from your DIY spreadsheets.

The main disadvantages of using software are:

- **Your training time**. It is easy to underestimate how much time it takes to get used to a new software package. It may take you all day to get the software set up and several days training to get up and running. This is, of course, all time that is not spent on growing your business.

- **Garbage in/Garbage out**. Just because the data is in the computer doesn't mean you have keyed it in correctly, set it up right or put it in the right place.

- **Processing time**. It may actually take longer to process each transaction in order to generate all the management information the software produces. And some of this information may not be very useful to a small business.

- **Flexibility**. Spreadsheets are by their nature infinitely flexible. You may not be able to do exactly what you want with some of the more basic accounting software packages.

- **Understanding**. If you don't understand the software it can be a lot more confusing than using the simple bookkeeping techniques outlined above.

Which Software Package?

There are many accounting packages for small businesses and virtually all of these are now monthly "cloud" subscriptions. There are surprisingly few desktop options left, not least because software companies want monthly payments rather than customers who buy licences and don't update their software for a number of years.

The main players in the UK accounting software market are as follows:

- Xero
- Quickbooks
- FreeAgent
- Sage
- Kashflow

Plus there are another 20 or so 'other' packages out there. All of these have their strengths and weaknesses and, as the features change quite quickly, it is hard to say anything meaningful in terms of comparisons. Generally they all do much the same thing and, when one innovates, the others quickly catch up.

The main advance in cloud accounting products is that they now usually link into your bank account and automatically import the statements. This means that there is usually less data entry required compared with legacy desktop software, and most of them "learn" what transactions might be and can make semi-automatic postings for you.

Other advantages include things like integrated billing, which allows the invoices you send out to customers to appear automatically in your accounts, online storage of purchase receipts to help with your filing, and even 'bot' credit control routines which send out reminders to customers who haven't paid their bills.

Finally, most of the products can be expanded with applications which (for a fee) can be used to do things like collect credit card payments or integrate your bookkeeping with other applications like website shopping carts. This means that the average business person with some basic IT knowledge can do things that even five years ago would have been in the realms of 'serious' IT development.

Which One Is Best?

There is no right answer. A lot depends on what you feel comfortable with. The good news is that most of the big brands do the job perfectly well, so if you just pick one that seems to cover all the features you want, you won't go too far wrong. Do however look beyond any "special offers" to what the final monthly price will be; cloud software is not something you tend to switch around very often.

What do our clients use? Well, in my own practice dealing primarily with smaller businesses in the service sector, Xero was our default software for several years but we are increasingly looking at Quickbooks Online given the much lower monthly fees. Compared to clients using older desktop versions of Quickbooks or Sage I would say we have achieved considerable time savings for both our clients and ourselves using cloud products.

We have quite a number of clients who like FreeAgent, which is aimed at contractors and very small services business.

One issue to consider is the package your accountant or bookkeeper is most familiar with, as you are likely to receive better quality ad hoc advice and pay less in fees by using something that easily fits in with their way of doing things. Often discounts are available if you buy through your accountant...so remember to ask nicely to have some of this passed on to you!

Finally, a word of caution from my professional life: generally speaking, I find that where clients have started using accounting software before speaking to their accountant, a lot of time can be spent doing remedial work, taking apart bad working practices. So if necessary get help to do it right first time.

If you are ready for software you probably have a big enough business to warrant paying for a bit of professional help, and this will help you get more out of your investment in terms of management information and data accuracy.

Chapter 34

Your First Employee

Not all small businesses employ someone from the start but in this chapter I outline the main practical issues when taking on your first employee.

The Basics

As you are probably aware, if you have been employed in the past, employers are responsible for the deduction of taxes from their employees before payment. This is called 'Pay as You Earn' (PAYE).

No doubt you've seen a big chunk of your wages disappear through income tax and national insurance payments.

What you may not realise is that, as an employer, you have to pay another amount on top for 'employer's national insurance'. The rate is 13.8% for 2018/19, although there is no employer's national insurance on the first £8,424 of salary.

In other words, if you pay someone a salary of £24,000 per annum you have to pay an extra £2,149 per year in national insurance. This is a tax deductible business expense.

The good news is that the first £3,000 of your employer's national insurance is met by the Government thanks to the Employment Allowance, so you may well find you don't actually pay any employer's NI on your first one or two staff members.

There is also no employer's national insurance on salaries paid to under 21s and apprentices under 25, provided, in both cases, salaries do not exceed £46,350 in 2018/19.

The PAYE Process

The following is an overview of the system:

- **Registration**. All new employers have to register with HMRC. This includes sole traders, partnerships and limited companies.

  Note that if you are a sole trader without any employees, you are the 'proprietor', not an employee, and therefore don't have to register.

  HMRC give links on how to register on their website, and encourage you to register online.

  www.gov.uk/register-employer

  Registering by phone is still possible by calling the new employer's helpline on 0300 200 3211.

- **Filing under RTI.** PAYE filing occurs under an online system called 'Real Time Information'. This is a system that collects detailed information about employees pay on a monthly basis. This system links into the Universal Credit, so care is required to ensure you do not make a mistake that affects your employee's benefits. In order to operate payroll you will either need to use HMRC's "Basic Tools" or a software provider. You can no longer submit paper returns for PAYE.

- **Set up**. Once you have registered with HMRC you will receive various guidance notes which should explain your first steps in adding your employees to the payroll.

- **Payslips**. Every month (or week if you are feeling particularly masochistic) you will pay your employee and hand across a payslip showing all the income tax and national insurance deductions you have made on their behalf. You are supposed to only pay your employees *after* the information about their pay has been transmitted to HMRC via the RTI system.

- **Tax payment**. As a small employer you may only need to make quarterly payments of the income tax and national insurance you have been deducting, plus your payments of employer's national insurance. The limit for quarterly payments is having an amount due of less than £1,500 per month.

- **Annual Returns**. You will need to supply employees with a P60 summarising their total pay and tax deductions for the year, and a P11D if you provide any benefits such as healthcare or a company car.

This is a good place to start for further guidance:

www.gov.uk/paye-for-employers/paye-and-payroll

The 'Basic PAYE Tools' for filing your online returns can be downloaded here, although do be warned, it is really quite horrible and you may do better using third party software:

www.gov.uk/basic-paye-tools

Who Should Carry Out the Payroll?

Generally speaking I wouldn't advise any small business to run its own payroll for three reasons:

- It is a complicated and time-consuming process if you don't know what you're doing.

- It doesn't cost much to get an accountant or specialist payroll provider to do it for you. Some firms will complete a small payroll for as little as £10-20 a month (although watch out for hidden fees!)

- Payroll is by its nature a sensitive subject. It's essential to have it processed correctly, so that you can explain to your employees why various deductions have been made.

Due to the bewildering number of obscure rules and regulations it is easy to make mistakes, especially with items such as sick pay, maternity pay, student loan deductions etc. If mistakes do occur most employers end up 'making good' any errors out of their own pockets, which could be costly. Even some accountants shy away from doing PAYE, unless they have an in-house specialist, as it's a full-time job keeping up with all the rule changes.

Giving the job to a small payroll provider should only cost you a few pounds per month and will certainly save a lot of time and stress.

If you really want to do it yourself, then the best way is to follow the instructions on the HMRC website step by step. These instructions are quite good, and the free New Employer's Helpline is also staffed by pretty competent people.

Some of the better accounting packages also offer payroll functionality, although this normally comes with an annual fee. One good value stand alone package worth looking at is Moneysoft's "Payroll Manager". There are also lots of cloud-based offerings springing up that can file all the necessary paperwork for fairly minimal cost, rather than using HMRC's "basic tools" which are quite basic!

Workplace Pensions Schemes (Auto Enrolment)

Compulsory workplace pensions have been phased in over the last few years, and from October 2017, all new employers have immediate auto-enrolment duties as soon as their PAYE duties begin.

Exemptions

There is an automatic enrolment exemption for "director only" limited companies, where the company has only one director and no other staff, or a number of directors and no other staff, but no more than one of the directors has an employment contract.

This means company owners generally cannot appoint their employees as directors to sidestep their pension obligations.

206

If automatic enrolment does not apply to your business, you will still have to notify the Pension Regulator:

www.thepensionsregulator.gov.uk/employers/What-if-I-dont-have-any-staff.aspx

Only employees earning more than £10,000 and aged from 22 to state pension age need to be *automatically* enrolled into a workplace pension.

However, some older and younger employees and those who earn less than £10,000 also have workplace pension rights:

- If an employee earns less than £6,032 for 2018/19 they don't need to be automatically enrolled but the employer has to give them access to a pension if they request it and if they are aged between 16 and 74. However, the employer is not required to contribute.

- If an employee earns between £6,032 and £10,000 and their age is between 16 and 74 they don't need to be automatically enrolled but do have the right to opt in. If they do decide to join the pension scheme the employer will have to contribute as well.

- If an employee earns more than £10,000 but is aged 16-21 or between state pension age and 74 they don't need to be automatically enrolled but do have the right to opt in. If they do decide to join the pension scheme the employer will have to contribute as well.

The Basics of Auto Enrolment

Under auto enrolment the central thrust is your employees are automatically enrolled into the pension scheme and only they can "opt out".

The idea behind this compulsion is very simple. A pension scheme is one of those things most people think they ought to have, yet many would put off actually doing anything about it.

By making employees actively opt out, precisely those people who trust their financial affairs more to luck than planning will probably end up in a scheme. They may only be in due to inertia but in they will be. Those people who are more hands on managing their affairs can make an active choice of staying in or opting out.

It's an elegant solution; it is also very annoying for the employer to administrate in practice, given the need to deal with all the opting in and opting out.

The basic steps are:

1. Register a scheme and chose a pension fund provider
2. Enrol your qualifying employees
3. As part of your regular payroll process, deduct pension contributions from your employees' pay
4. Every 3 years you must enrol any employees that opted out earlier

You can see from step 4, the architects of this scheme really are keen on getting people to pay into a pension!

The main source of help in this area is the Pensions Regulator's website, so if your business is affected I would start there for background research:

www.thepensionsregulator.gov.uk

Most employers will then need to get some professional help beyond this book, typically from an independent financial advisor, accountant or payroll provider, or possibly a combination of these.

One further thing to note is the direct financial cost to the employer. Not only do employers need to wade through a considerable amount of paperwork to open and maintain a scheme, they also have to make a cash contribution to the pension too.

The current employer contribution rate is 2% on qualifying earnings, but this goes up to 3% from 6 April 2019. This is on top of the existing employer's national insurance contributions of 13.8%.

The employee contribution is 3% in 2018/19 and 5% from April 2019.

General Tips for New Employers

- Get help interviewing candidates – a lot of recruitment companies will help you interview and select the best candidate for a role. If you only have one or two members of staff, selecting the best candidate is vital to your new business.

- Get a proper contract. The rapid changes in employment law over the past few years have been significant and nearly all in favour of the employee. Having a good contract can save a lot of time and money in the event of a dispute. Don't be tempted to use something you find free on the web.

- Employer's indemnity insurance is not only compulsory if you have employees but can be very handy if, as a small business, you transgress some of the myriad of employment rules.

Contractors vs Employees

Given the level of red tape, the legal responsibilities and the cost of employing someone, lots of small businesses now prefer to use contractors rather than employ someone to carry out a specific task.

The cost tends to be higher but you should generally only pay for the time you use and there is no PAYE to worry about or additional taxation.

Contractors can be helpful when your business has seasonal peaks and troughs or just to add depth to a team where the business is too small to take on a full-time specialist.

The dividing line between employees and contractors can become quite blurred but there is often scope to define the relationship to give the desired result.

For example, let's say Raj needs a part-time secretary. He calls a local secretarial service and books someone for two hours a day.

However, sometimes there is no work to do and sometimes there is extra work available. Raj pays for the hours worked. One day the secretary accidentally orders 1,000 reams of paper instead of 10. The secretarial service agrees to sort this out with the stationery company for free as it was their employee's error. This sort of arrangement is indicative of a contractor relationship.

Raj's friend Colin also needs a part-time secretary. He places an advert in the local paper for a PA to come in for two hours a day.

He interviews three candidates and chooses the best one. If there is no work to do, he still has to pay the hours arranged. His secretary also has a bad day with the paper supplies but in this instance Colin has to pay overtime to cover time spent resolving the problem. This sort of arrangement is indicative of an employee relationship as Colin is taking on more of the risks of employment, rather than paying on a 'results' basis.

In these two examples it is quite clear cut who is who. In real life you may well need to take advice as to whether people who work in your business are contractors or employees.

HMRC scrutinise these situations quite carefully because there is potential to pay quite a lot less tax by defining a relationship as a contractor rather than an employee. In cases where it is found that the person really was an employee it is generally the employer who has to pay the additional tax. It is therefore very much in your interests as a small business to get the status clarified.

Chapter 35

How to Choose an Accountant or Bookkeeper

Throughout this book I have tried to point out areas where you may benefit from professional help. If you have never used an accountant before – and this probably applies to 90% of people with a new business – it can be daunting wondering what to expect, how much to pay and how to differentiate between different accountants and bookkeepers.

Accountants vs Bookkeepers

Q. What's the difference between an accountant and a bookkeeper?
A. About £100 an hour.

Jokes aside, this is actually a serious point. Although there is quite a lot of overlap between the two roles there are also some profound differences that may not be immediately apparent.

The bookkeeper will add up the numbers but a good accountant will know what numbers need adding up in the first place, and what to do with them once they are compiled. It is the difference between having an operational role and a management one.

Figure 35.1 shows the rough and by no means comprehensive division of tasks each will undertake.

A good bookkeeper will be diligent, accurate and quick. Moreover, good bookkeepers also know their limits. It's a 'good thing' if you ask your bookkeeper to do something and he or she tells you that an accountant normally does this particular task. This means they aren't trying to take on anything beyond their experience.

Most of the tasks covered in this book could be carried out by a good bookkeeper, although many would probably not be willing to help you choose a VAT scheme, for example.

Figure 35.1 Accountants vs Bookkeepers

Bookkeeper	Accountant
Day-to-day record keeping	Direct what records to keep
Input data into accounting system	Help you select accounting system, set it up and adapt to your changing needs
Prepare VAT and PAYE returns	Checking VAT and PAYE returns, and provide a point of contact to discuss new situations or trickier issues
Collation of records for the year end to pass to an accountant.	Preparation of final accounts, year-end adjustments, tax computation and returns.
Advice about keeping paperwork and other day-to-day issues	Broader advice about the direction of your business, things to keep an eye on, tax-planning opportunities. Buying or selling a business.

I would be wary if a bookkeeper offered help on tax matters such as completing your tax return, unless you have very simple affairs.

Nearly all bookkeepers will be able to competently transfer the numbers from your records into your tax return – the question is whether they are using the right numbers and understand enough about tax to do it correctly.

What bookkeepers are great for, however, is removing some of the drudgery of business red tape. A lot of people just aren't cut out to do this type of work and getting a good bookkeeper on board can result in a dramatic improvement in the quality of your record keeping and free you up to spend time on more productive tasks within your business.

I do, however, think it's important for every small business owner to keep a keen interest in their records, even if they are being looked after by a bookkeeper. This way you can keep a handle on how much you are spending, which customers haven't paid, what stock you have and other vital management information.

A good accountant will always make time for you, understand your type of business and the challenges you face. Small business owners often develop very close relationships with their accountants, who may be their only 'professional' adviser and business confidant.

Although one of the basic tasks for any accountant is to prepare your tax return and calculate the right amount of tax, this shouldn't be where the relationship ends.

The more effort you put into getting to know your accountant, the more you should get out of the relationship. I know from my own practice that I have very little input into the general business affairs of those clients I only speak to once a year. Those clients I have contact with on a regular basis tend to enjoy a far better level of service, as I am able to acquire a good understanding of their businesses. This way I can give timely advice and suggestions.

A quick two-line email to your accountant when something in your business changes will result in either reassurance that 'everything's OK' or immediate action. Where I don't see things until the end of the year, there is usually little time to be proactive – only time for damage limitation, which generally means more cost for the client.

Do I Need an Accountant?

There is no legal obligation to appoint an accountant, unless your business turnover is quite large and you need to have a 'statutory audit' carried out. The current audit threshold is turnover of £10.2 million.

Practically speaking, you should almost certainly get an accountant if you have a limited company or are VAT-registered. You may also benefit substantially as a sole trader, just from being able to sleep at night knowing that your records are in good order and your tax return has been accurately completed. In most cases your accountant will probably also save you a slice off your tax bill too.

Qualifications

Unfortunately, there is a bewildering array of professional qualifications in the accounting world. This is partly because, unlike solicitors, anyone can legally call themselves an 'accountant', and partly due to the failure of the various accounting bodies to form one entity.

Bookkeepers

Some really good bookkeepers are 'unqualified' or 'qualified by experience' (QBEs). This isn't necessarily a bad thing, especially for the mature person who may have trained years ago when passing exams wasn't as common.

Many bookkeepers who have trained in the past 10 to 15 years will have studied for the 'AAT'. This is in four levels:

1. Bookkeeping Certificate (basic understanding of bookkeeping)
2. Foundation
3. Intermediate
4. Technician (Good rounded understanding of accounting)

Find out which level your bookkeeper has got to, as there is a huge gap from top to bottom. I would generally look for Intermediate or above as a mark of general competence to independently offer bookkeeping services.

Having said that, one of the most important qualities you should be looking for is experience in your type of business. Although it sounds harsh, a 'newly qualified' bookkeeper (or accountant for that matter) will be on a steep learning curve... rather let them learn on someone else's books!

Chartered Accountants

There are three major accounting bodies in the UK:

- ACCA – Association of Chartered Certified Accountants

- ICAEW – Institute of Chartered Accountants in England and Wales

- ICAS – Institute of Chartered Accountants of Scotland

These are the only three institutes whose members can call themselves 'chartered accountants'.

Members of these bodies will usually have the following letters after their names: ACCA, ACA, or CA. They may also have FCA or FCCA, with the 'F' standing for Fellow and indicating that the member has possibly more experience (although many experienced accountants don't bother applying to become FCAs or FCCAs).

As with every profession, there is quite a bit of professional rivalry and snobbery. The ACAs tend to look down their noses at ACCAs. Quite frankly, for a small business it doesn't matter too much what type of chartered accountant you go for. They've all sat much the same exams and broadly will have much the same knowledge as each other, although knowledge will depend very much on the experience they have had through training and since qualification.

There are several other accountancy bodies. The two main ones are:

- CIPFA – Public Sector Accountants (working in Government)

- CIMA – Management accountants (working in larger businesses)

It is rare for members of either of these two bodies to be 'in practice', offering their services directly to the public, and most would do the extra exams and be admitted to the ACCA if they wanted to switch career paths.

Opting for a chartered accountant ensures that your accountant:

- Has reached a high standard of academic study and is therefore reasonably bright.

- Has spent a bare minimum of three years qualifying and gained a further two years practical experience before being able to trade independently.

- Has studied a broad range of relevant material and has carried out mandatory ongoing training to keep up to date with new material.

- Has professional indemnity insurance, so you know that if you make a claim for bad advice they will have the funds to pay for your losses.

- Is subject to a good complaints procedure. Professional reputations are important for the institutes, and they therefore make a public show of ensuring accountants play fair and do a good job.

What you won't know is:

- The accountant's specific experience.

- What environment they trained in (for example, big business, smaller business, the public sector, manufacturing etc).

- How much they charge and on what basis.

- Whether you will get on with them personally.

- Whether your chosen accountant is any good, despite having the necessary qualifications. As with everything in life you get good and bad accountants.

Other Accountants

As well as Chartered Accountants, there are also lot of other accountants who are not members of a chartered body and offer much the same services as those that are. As above anyone at all can quite legally describe themselves as an accountant. This is a tricky area to explain, as having a practicing certificate from a chartered institute does NOT automatically make you better than someone who does not. Indeed there are lots of reputable hard working accountants out there who are not Chartered Accountants but will do an excellent job for you and some terrible Chartered Accountants who won't.

The key thing to remember when looking at 'other' accountants is that there is no pre-selection. It's a bit like buying a used car as a private sale rather than a dealer. Whilst you might well inadvertently buy a dodgy car from a dealer, it's far more likely to happen with a private individual so you need to make more of an effort to check what you are buying as there is unlikely to be a warranty attached. In the second car world there are of course lots of honest private sellers, just as there are lots of competent accountants who don't happen to be Chartered so don't dismiss them out of hand, but do tread carefully.

Do find out for example if they have ever been a member of an institute and the reasons for leaving (there is a big difference between someone fed up of paying the subs and someone who has been expelled!), do check they have proper Professional Indemnity Insurance and do check out their level of knowledge and experience and look for strong recommendations. It's very much 'buyer beware'.

What I will say however is you find a good accountant hang onto them and don't worry too much what paperwork they have up on the wall.

Choosing an Accountant and Bookkeeper

Although you will get some idea of an individual's competence by looking at his or her qualifications, what this won't tell you is how enthusiastic, skilled or hardworking that person is.

As a rule of thumb you should choose an accountant with a business similar in size to your own. In other words, if you are a sole trader, there is little point asking one of the larger firms to act for you. They won't be used to small business issues, will charge a lot more and you are unlikely to get much one-to-one time with your accountant as 99% of the work will be completed by juniors.

Similarly, if you are a medium-sized business with several offices, you probably won't benefit from using a one-man band, as they are unlikely to have the resources or experience to cope with your needs. Instead use a medium-sized firm with experience dealing with similar sized businesses.

The next step is to ask around and see who has a good reputation and then set up a meeting, either on the telephone or in person. Most accountants will offer a free initial consultation to go over your affairs, and this is your opportunity to sound out their knowledge, experience and working practices.

Make sure you speak to several accountants until you find one that you get along with – remember you want to develop a long-term business relationship with this person.

Fees for smaller enterprises are usually set on a 'fixed fee' basis. This means that you are being charged for a job to be completed, rather than on an hourly basis.

This tends to work well for routine paperwork such as completing tax returns but less well for the provision of advice where the scope may be less clearly defined. Advice tends to still be charged on an hourly basis and will usually be completed by one of the more senior members of staff.

Routine tax return work will generally be completed by either trainees or in-house assistants. Returns are then checked by an accountant before they are issued and discussed with you. Only in very small practices will the qualified accountant actually carry out all the routine paperwork.

The danger for a small business using a larger firm of accountants is that you may be pushed aside by bigger clients, which is why it is often helpful to match your business to the size of the accounting firm so you are always 'core business' and not on the periphery.

218

I should point out that some of the larger regional firms maintain very good small business departments, which can give the feel of a small practice despite being part of a larger firm. So explore what's on offer locally.

Once you have chosen a firm ask for all fees to be quoted in writing and check whether figures include VAT or not. You will probably receive an 'engagement letter' outlining the fees and terms for anything other than a very simple self-assessment return.

For hourly fees remember to ask for a fee cap – a maximum charge for a given piece of work. Although fixed fees may sometimes be negotiable, always bear in mind that accountants are selling their time, and if the fee is squeezed you may also find the service is squeezed too. Probably the most valuable service – tax planning and business support – is often the first thing to go with a cut-price deal.

Check-list for making an appointment

- ✓ Who is recommended?
- ✓ Do they hold relevant qualifications?
- ✓ Is it the right size of firm?
- ✓ Did they respond to my initial approach promptly?
- ✓ For larger firms, who will I actually be dealing with on a day-to-day basis?
- ✓ Do they have experience of my type and size of business?
- ✓ Am I happy with the fee structure?
- ✓ Am I 100% sure I get on with this person?

Dealing Day to Day with Your Adviser

It is worth remembering that your relationship with your accountant is a two way street.

Looking at it from the accountant's point of view, the following tips will help you get on with your adviser.

- **Keep good records**. If your records are poor, it will be cheaper to use a bookkeeper to sort them out than your accountant. Dumping a big pile of receipts on your accountant's doorstep will elicit a big groan and an even bigger bill.

- **Get in early**. Sole traders with a financial year ending in March, and tax returns not due until the end of January, 10 months later, often feel no sense of urgency to get their records over to their accountant. Remember, however, that accountants are very busy from November onwards, and many impose a 'busy season' premium for late delivery of information or discounts for early records.

  Not only will you probably pay more at this time of year, the quality of advice may be lower too as there is likely to be more time pressure on your accountant. If you get your accounts information together in early summer, you should find him only too keen to spend time working with you and some even offer 'early-bird' discounts.

- **Don't hold back**. Your accountant is there to help you. The more information you give, the better the advice that can be provided. Good accountants like communicative clients with whom they can get involved.

- **Respond to requests for information**. If you make your accountant wait weeks and chase you repeatedly for information it will ultimately result in higher bills – accountants make for an expensive diary reminder service.

- **Be realistic**. Although sometimes they can make your tax bill disappear, accountants cannot always perform such miracles, especially if you act first and ask questions later.

You should find that if you follow these tips you will end up with a positive business relationship which should mean in turn you get far better service in the longer term and better quality advice.

Headed Paper

The following notes outline the rules for headed paper. These vary depending on what business structure you have. Although there is no legal requirement to do so, I generally suggest to clients to treat their websites as an 'official document' and therefore include the same information.

For a sole trader you need:

- Your name (as proprietor)
- Any trading name
- Your trading address

If your trading name incorporates your name then this is not a problem. If I was a sole trader my trading name 'James Smith, Chartered Accountant' would be acceptable to cover both points.

For a limited company there is more information to include:

- You must include the company's full legal name
- Any trading names
- Where the company is registered i.e. England, Scotland or Northern Ireland
- Your correspondence address
- The registered company number
- The registered office address if different to your correspondence address
- Your VAT number if registered

Some of this information will quite naturally be included, i.e. the trading name and correspondence address. If you look at other people's headed paper you will probably see everything else in very small type on the bottom two lines. So long as it is legible this is perfectly acceptable practice.

My own footer for my practice runs as follows:

'James Smith, Chartered Accountant' is the trading name of James Smith (Accountant) Limited registered in England no. 4832439

Had my registered office address differed from my trading address I would simply add this in at the end to continue the flow.

HMRC Categories for Self Assessment

Table of allowable and disallowable expenses

(Taken from Self-employment (full) notes: Page SEFN 5 onward)

Box No. Number Long(Short)	Allowable Cost	Disallowable Cost
17 (11)	Cost of goods bought for re-sale, cost of raw materials used; direct costs of producing goods sold; adjustments for opening and closing stock and work in progress; commissions payable; discounts given.	Cost of goods or materials bought for private use; depreciation of equipment
18 (19)	Construction industry subcontractor payments (before taking off any tax)	Payments made for non-business work
19 (13)	Salaries, wages, bonuses, pensions, benefits for staff or employees; agency fees, subcontract labour costs; employer's NICs etc.	Own wages and drawings, pension payments or NIC contributions; payments made for non-business work
20 (12)	Car and van insurance, repairs, servicing, fuel, parking, hire charges, vehicle licence fees, motoring organisation membership; train, bus, air and taxi fares; hotel room costs and meals on overnight business trips	Non-business motoring costs (private use proportions); fines; costs of buying vehicles; travel costs between home and business; other meals
21 (14)	Rent for business premises, business and water rates, light, heat, power, property insurance, security, use of home as office (business proportion only)	Costs of any non-business part of premises; costs of buying business premises

22 (15)	Repairs and maintenance of business premises and equipment; renewals of small tools and items of equipment	Repairs of non-business parts of premises or equipment; costs of improving or altering premises and equipment
23 (18)	Telephone and fax running costs; postage, stationery, printing and small office equipment costs; computer software	Non-business or private use proportion of expenses; new telephone, fax, computer hardware or other equipment costs
24 (19)	Advertising in newspapers, directories etc., mailshots, free samples, website costs	Entertaining clients, suppliers and customers; hospitality at events
25 (17)	Interest on bank and other business loans; alternative finance payments	Repayment of loans; a proportion of interest and other charges if borrowing not used solely for the business.
26 (17)	Bank, overdraft and credit card charges; hire purchase interest and leasing payments; alternative finance payments	Repayment of loans; a proportion of interest and other charges if borrowing not used solely for the business.
27 (19)	Amounts included in turnover but unpaid and written off because they will not be recovered	Debts not included in turnover; debts relating to fixed assets; general bad debts
28 (16)	Accountant's, solicitor's, surveyor's, architect's and other professional fees; professional indemnity insurance premiums	Legal costs of buying property and large items of equipment; costs of settling tax disputes and fines for breaking the law
29 (n/a)	Depreciation and loss/profit on sale of assets are not allowable expenses – any amount entered here should also be entered in box 44	Depreciation of equipment, cars etc.; losses on sales of assets (minus any profits on sales)
30 (19)	Other expenses. Trade or professional journals and subscriptions; other sundry business running expenses not included elsewhere; net VAT payments	Payments to clubs, charities, political parties etc.; non-business part of any expenses; cost of ordinary clothing

Appendix Three

Flat Rate VAT Scheme Rates

Business Category	Headline Rate	Effective Rate
Limited cost trader	16.5%	19.8%
Accountancy or book-keeping	14.5%	17.4%
Advertising	11%	13.2%
Agricultural services	11%	13.2%
Any other activity not listed elsewhere	12%	14.4%
Architect, civil/structural engineer, surveyor	14.5%	17.4%
Boarding or care of animals	12%	14.4%
Business services not listed elsewhere	12%	14.4%
Catering including restaurants/takeaways	12.5%	15%
Computer/IT consultancy, data processing	14.5%	17.4%
Computer repair services	10.5%	12.6%
Dealing in waste or scrap	10.5%	12.6%
Entertainment or journalism	12.5%	15%
Estate agency, property management services	12%	14.4%
Farming or agriculture not listed elsewhere	6.5%	7.8%
Film, radio, television or video production	13%	15.6%
Financial services	13.5%	16.2%
Forestry or fishing	10.5%	12.6%
General building or construction services	9.5%	11.4%
Hairdressing, other beauty treatment services	13%	15.6%
Hiring or renting goods	9.5%	11.4%
Hotel or accommodation	10.5%	12.6%
Investigation or security	12%	14.4%
Labour-only building, construction services	14.5%	17.4%
Laundry or dry-cleaning services	12%	14.4%
Lawyer or legal services	14.5%	17.4%
Library, archive, museum, other cultural	9.5%	11.4%
Management consultancy	14%	16.8%
Manufacturing fabricated metal products	10.5%	12.6%
Manufacturing food	9%	10.8%
Manufacturing that is not listed elsewhere	9.5%	11.4%
Manufacturing yarn, textiles or clothing	9%	10.8%
Membership organisation	8%	9.6%
Mining or quarrying	10%	12%
Packaging	9%	10.8%
Photography	11%	13.2%

Business Category	Headline Rate	Effective Rate
Post offices	5%	6%
Printing	8.5%	10.2%
Publishing	11%	13.2%
Pubs	6.5%	7.8%
Real estate activity not listed elsewhere	14%	16.8%
Repairing personal or household goods	10%	12%
Repairing vehicles	8.5%	10.2%
Retailing food, confectionary, tobacco, newspapers, children's clothing	4%	4.8%
Retailing pharmaceuticals, medical goods, cosmetics or toiletries	8%	9.6%
Retailing that is not listed elsewhere	7.5%	9%
Retailing vehicles or fuel	6.5%	7.8%
Secretarial services	13%	15.6%
Social work	11%	13.2%
Sport or recreation	8.5%	10.2%
Transport or storage, including couriers, freight, removals and taxis	10%	12%
Travel agency	10.5%	12.6%
Veterinary medicine	11%	13.2%
Wholesaling agricultural products	8%	9.6%
Wholesaling food	7.5%	9%
Wholesaling that is not listed elsewhere	8.5%	10.2%